Flowers & Butterflies
Coloring Book For Girls

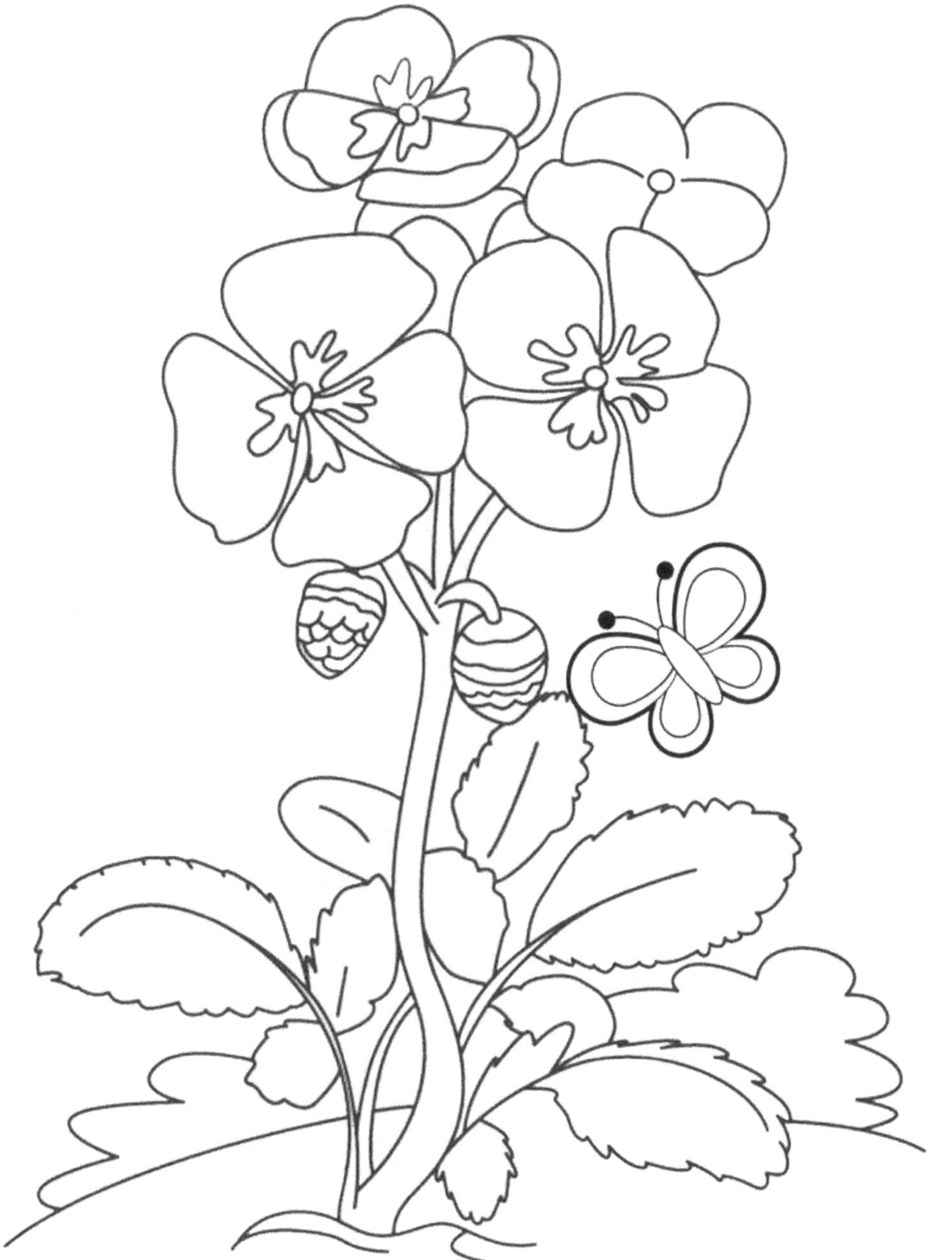

Flowers and Butterflies Coloring Book For Girls

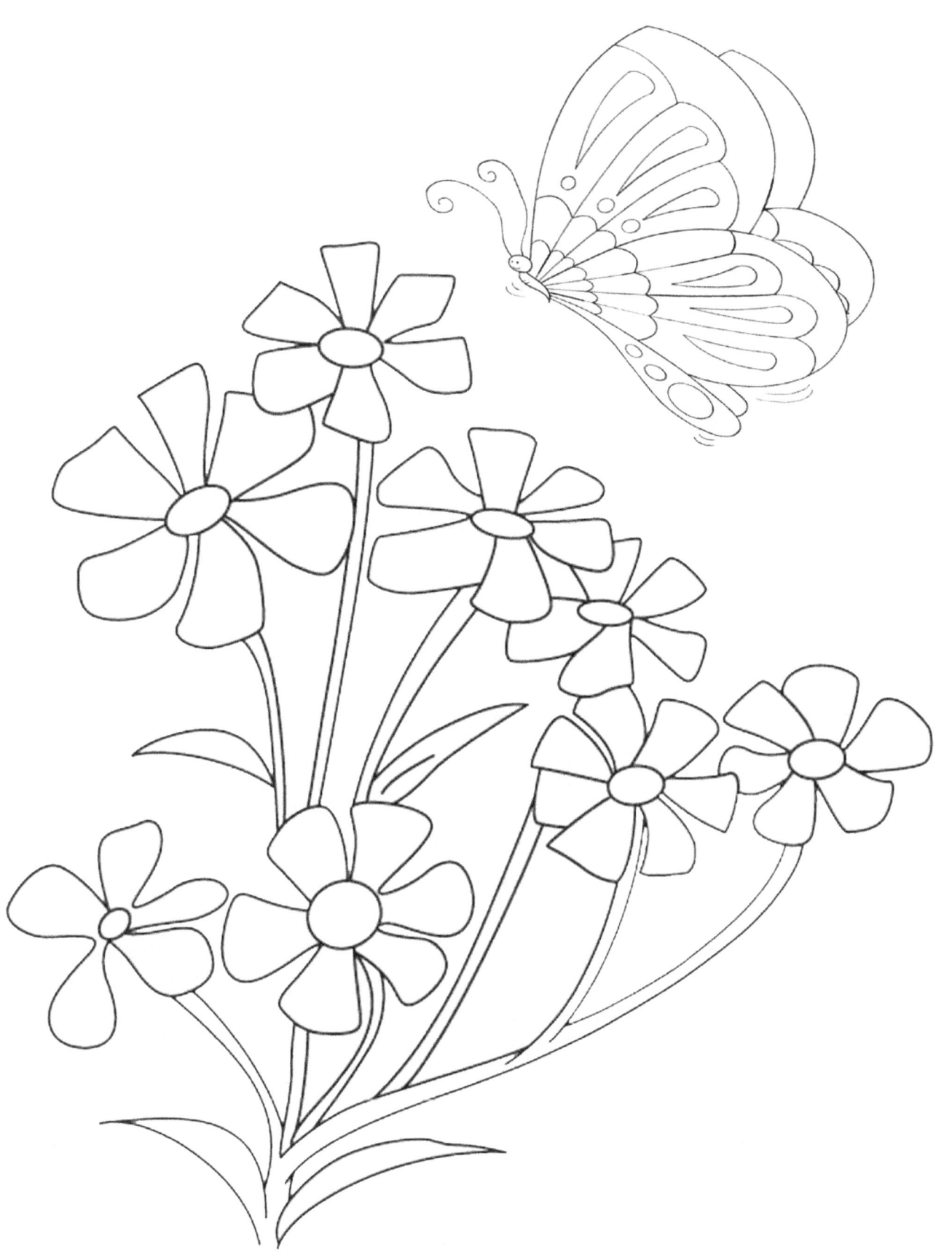

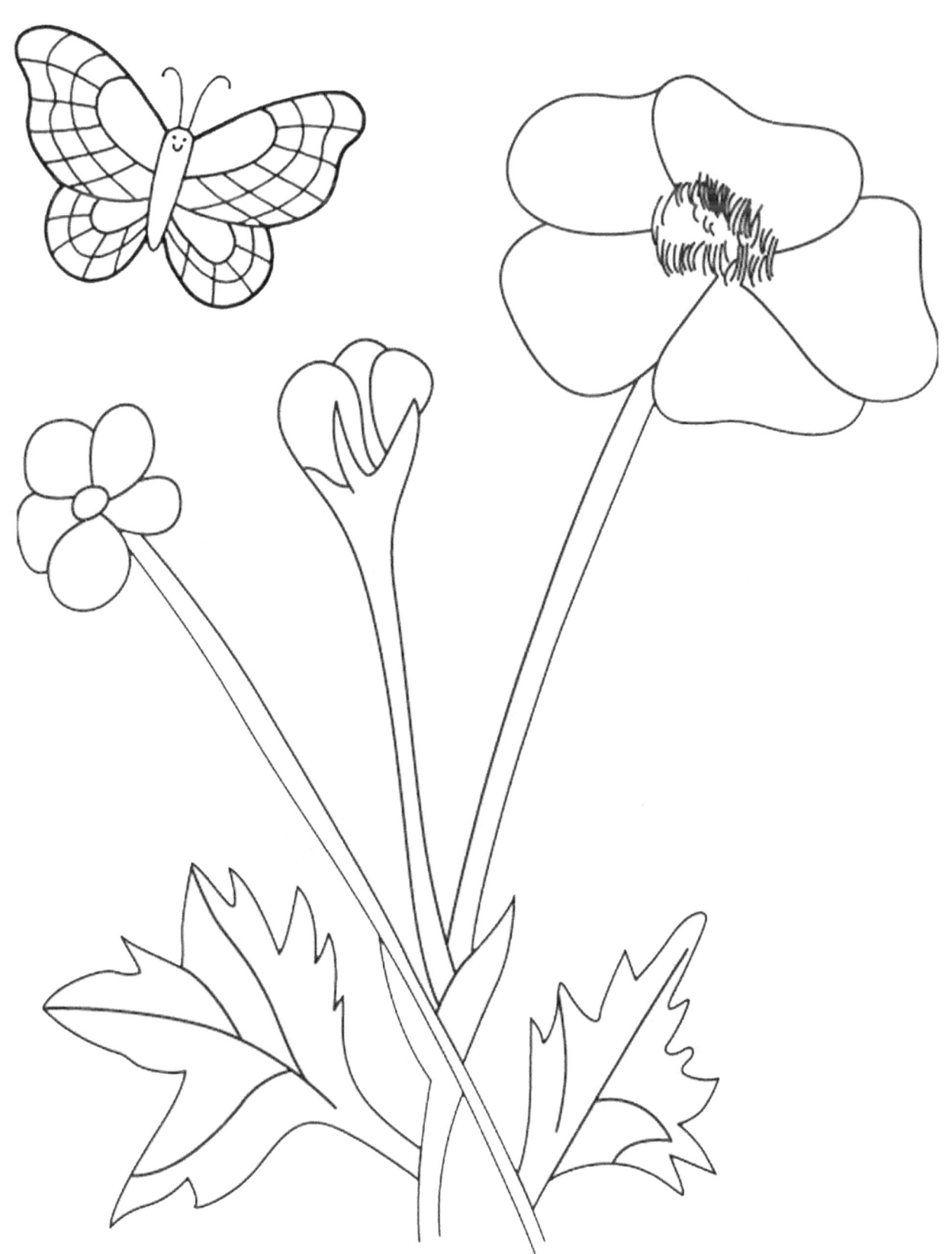

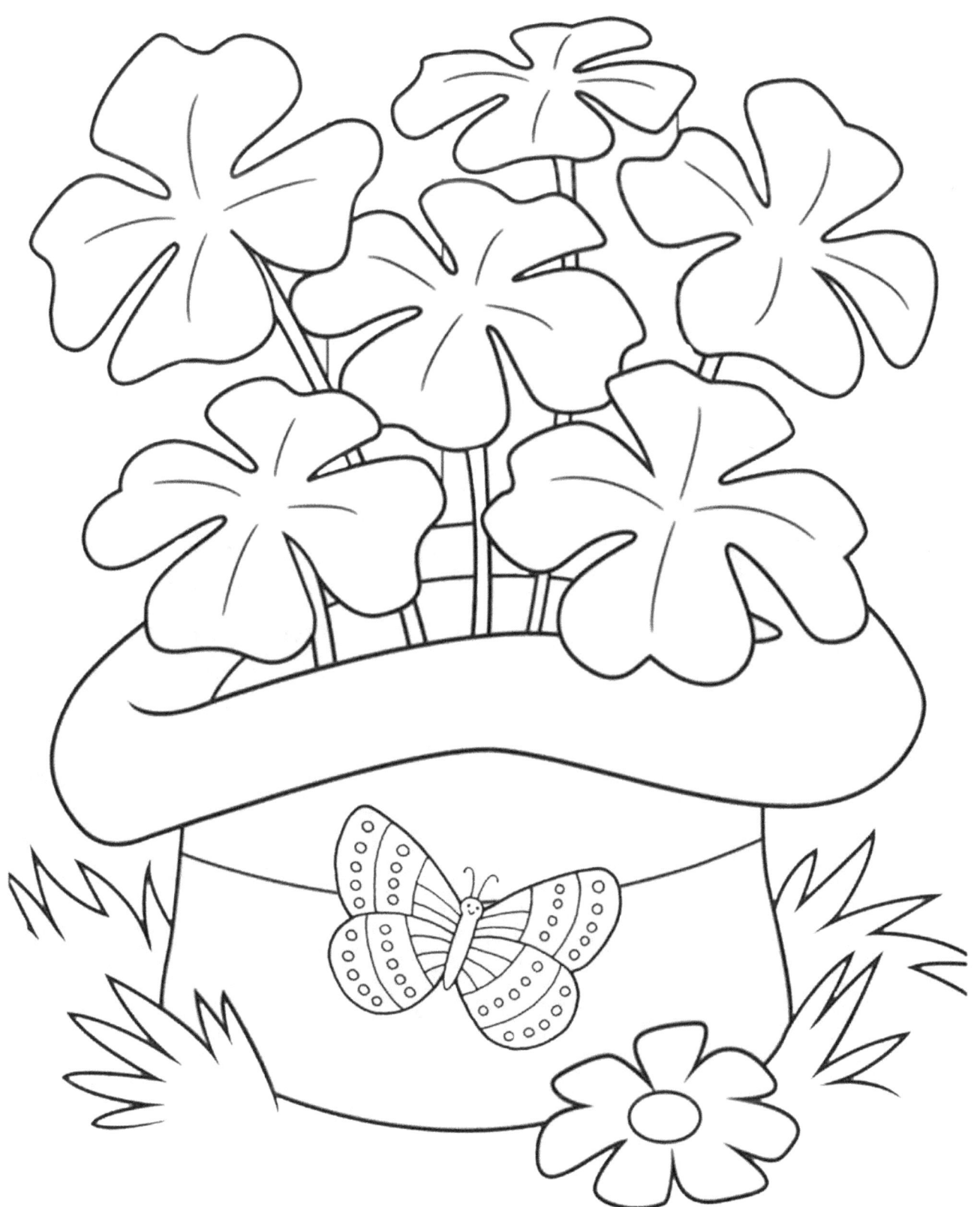

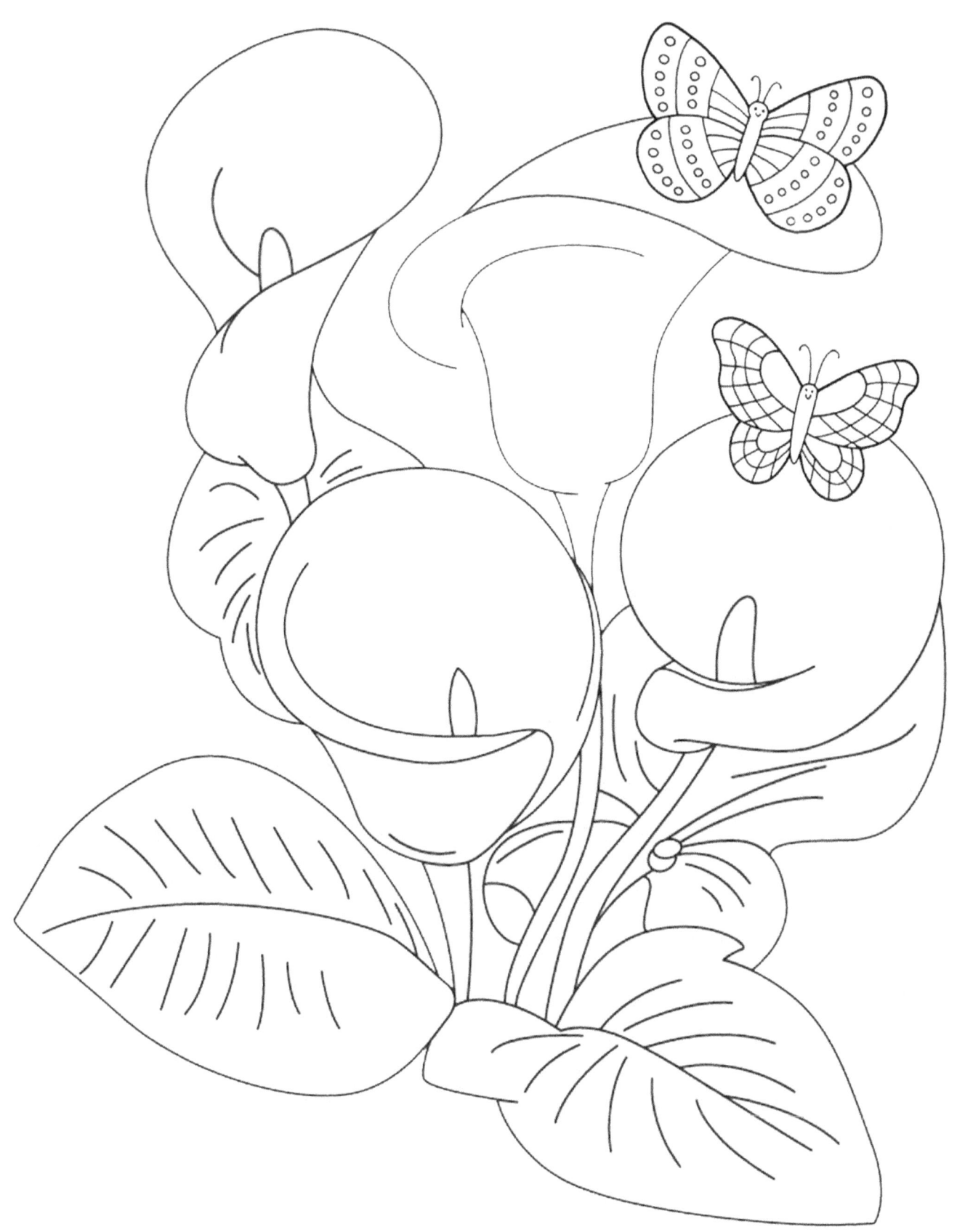

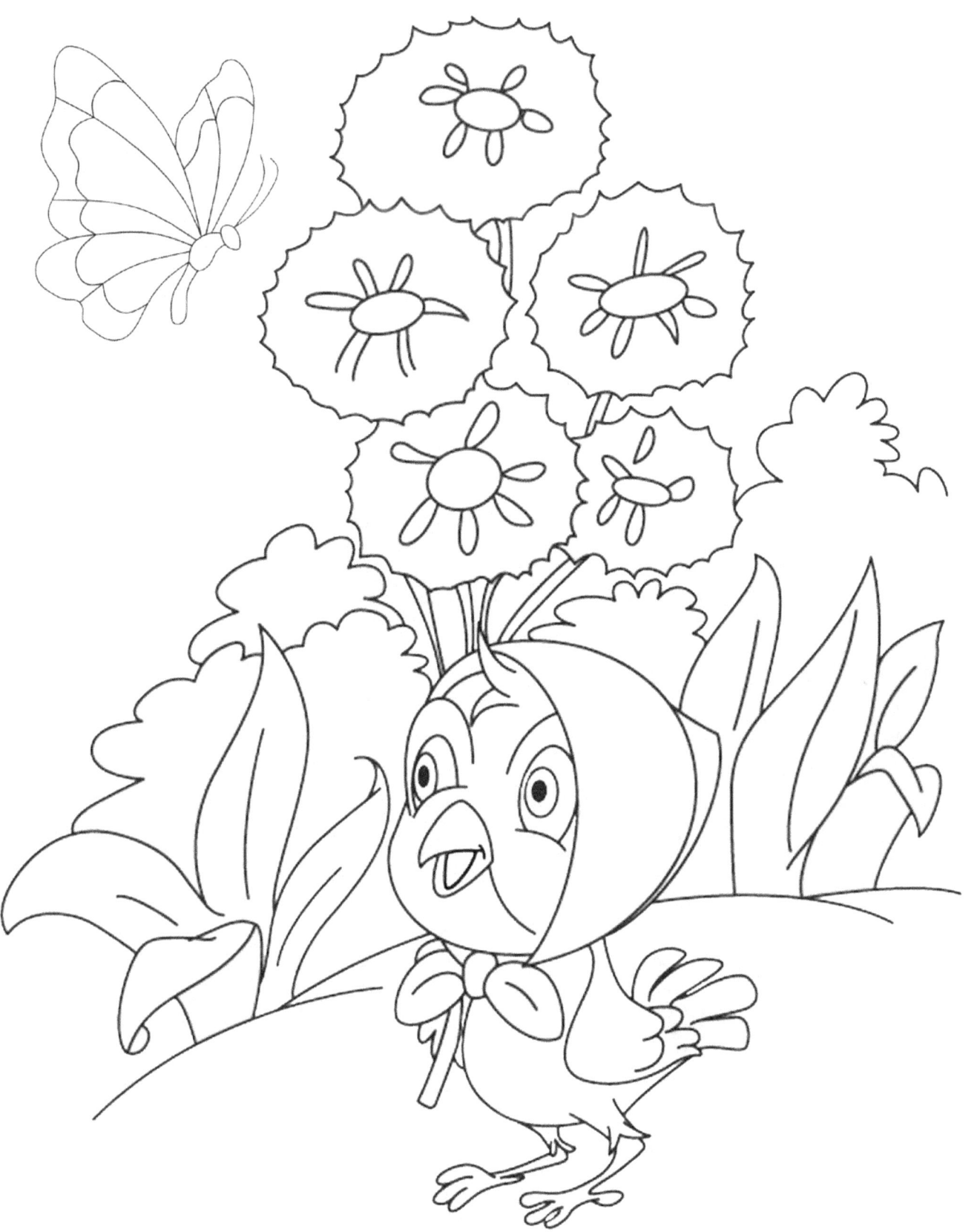

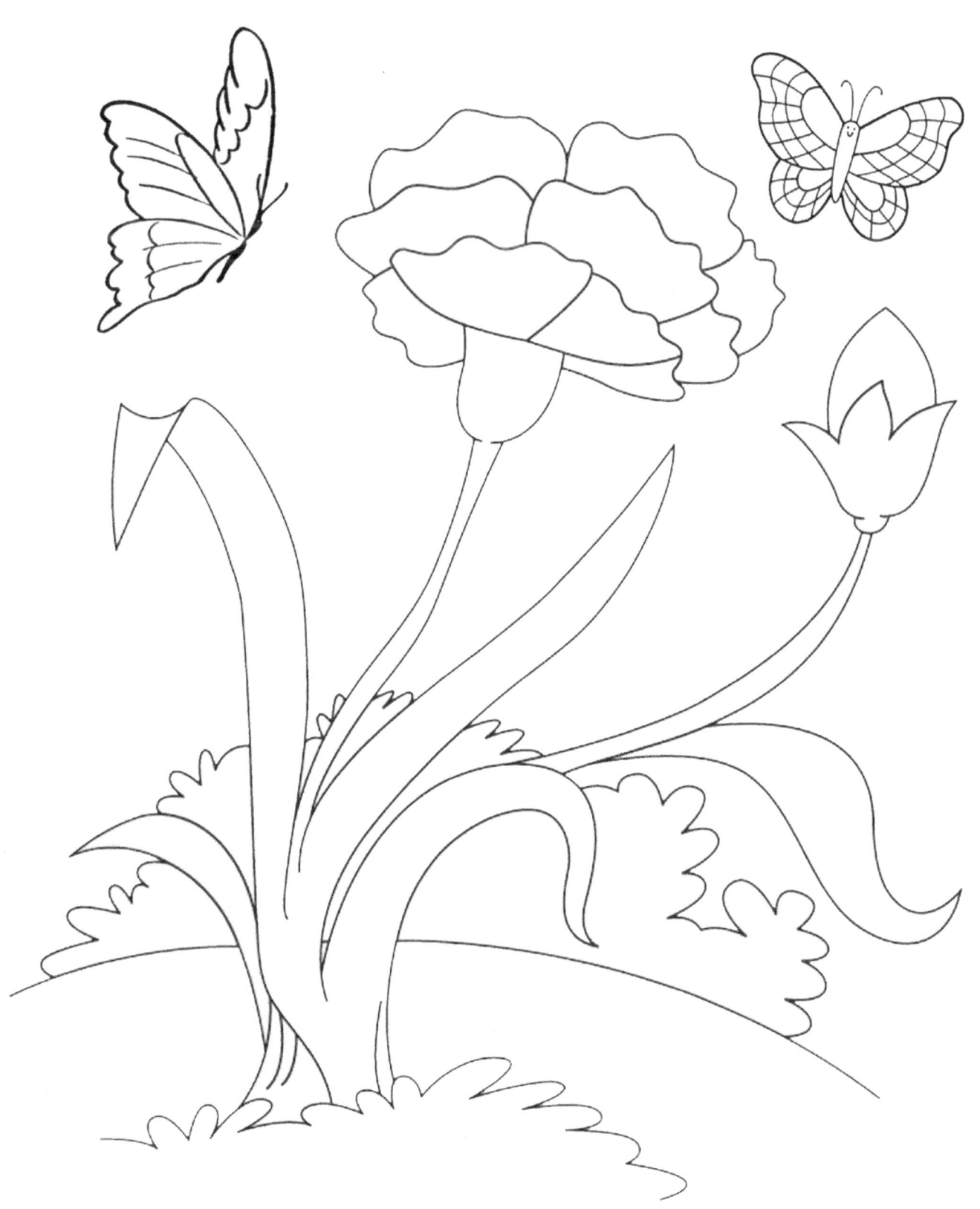

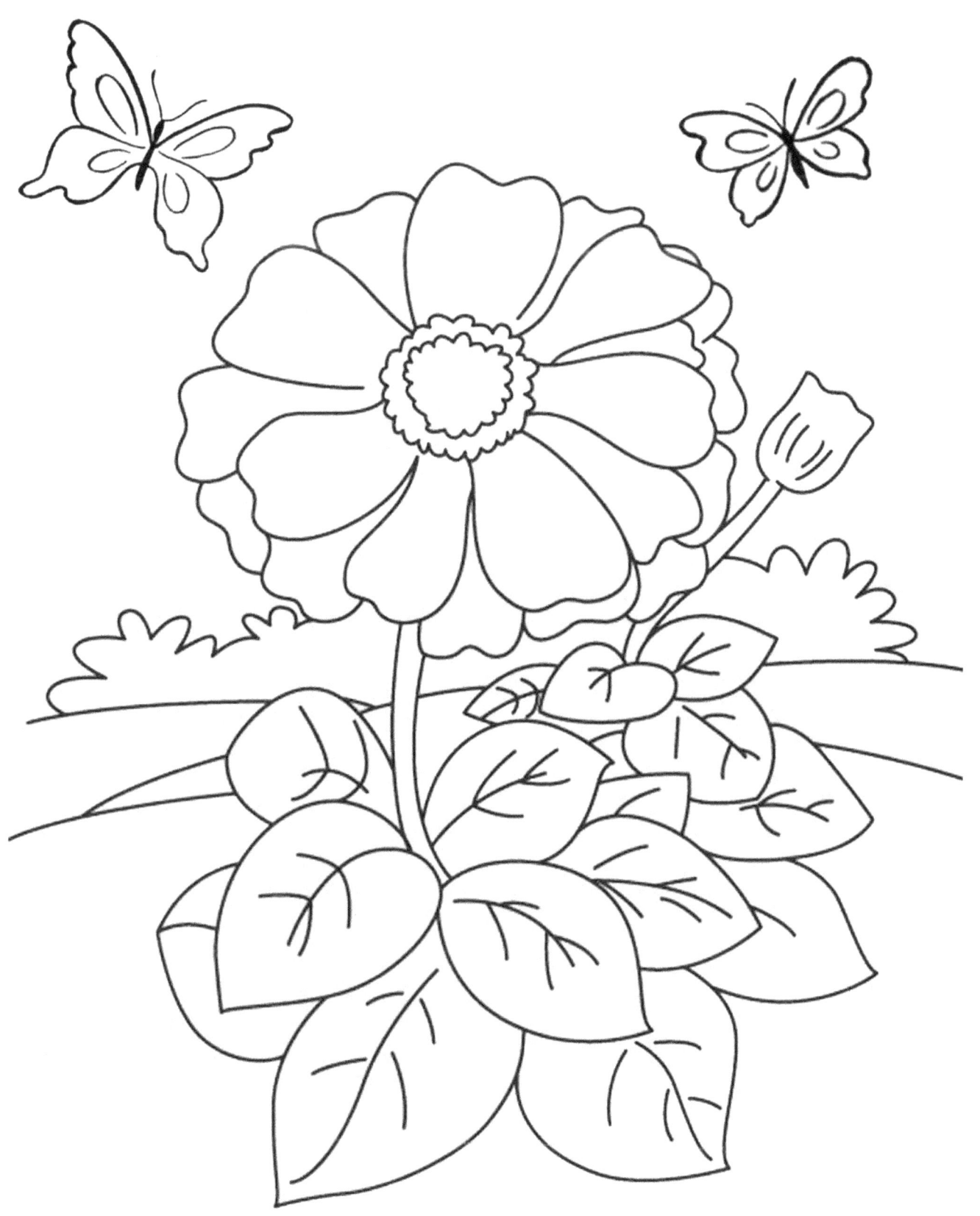

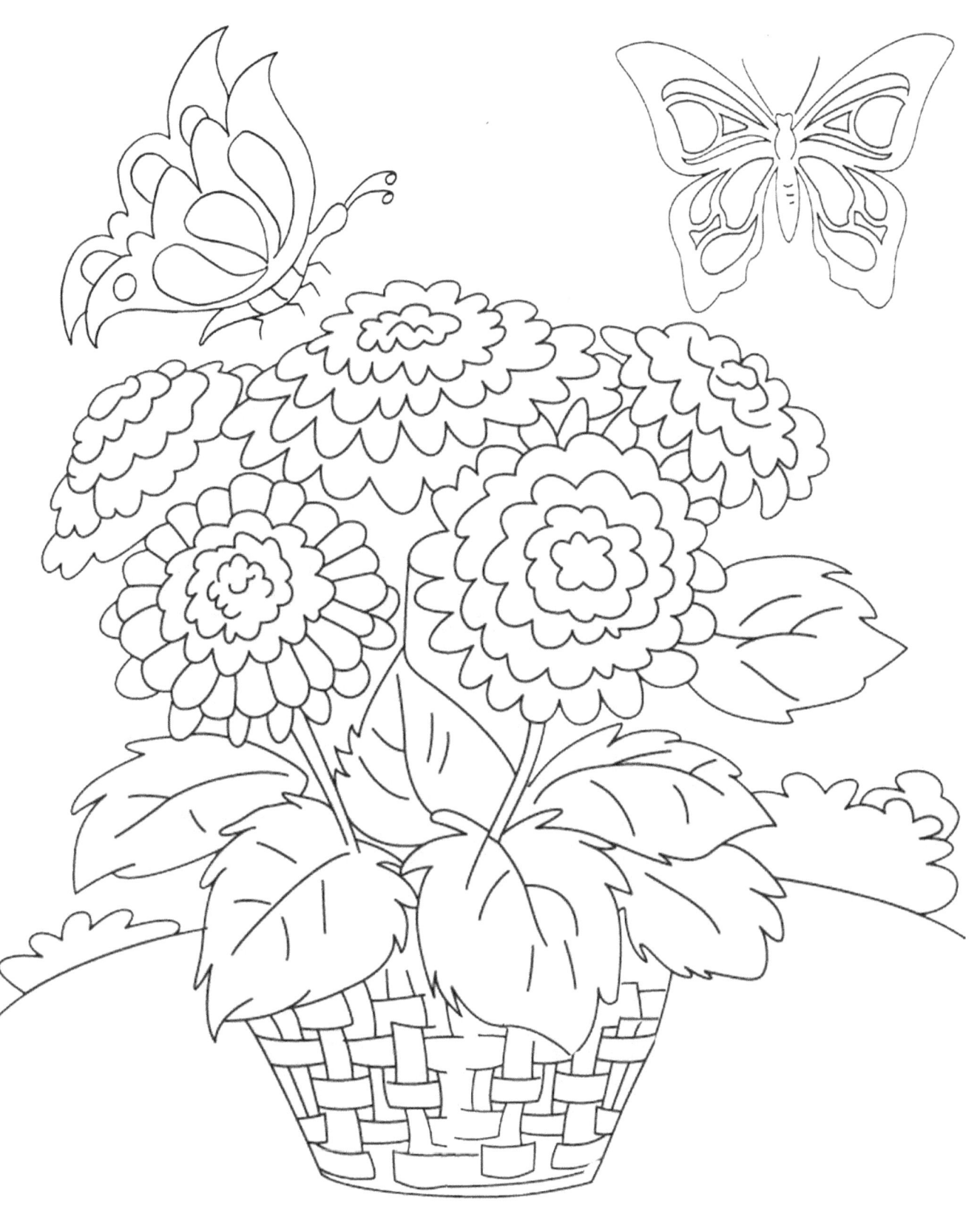

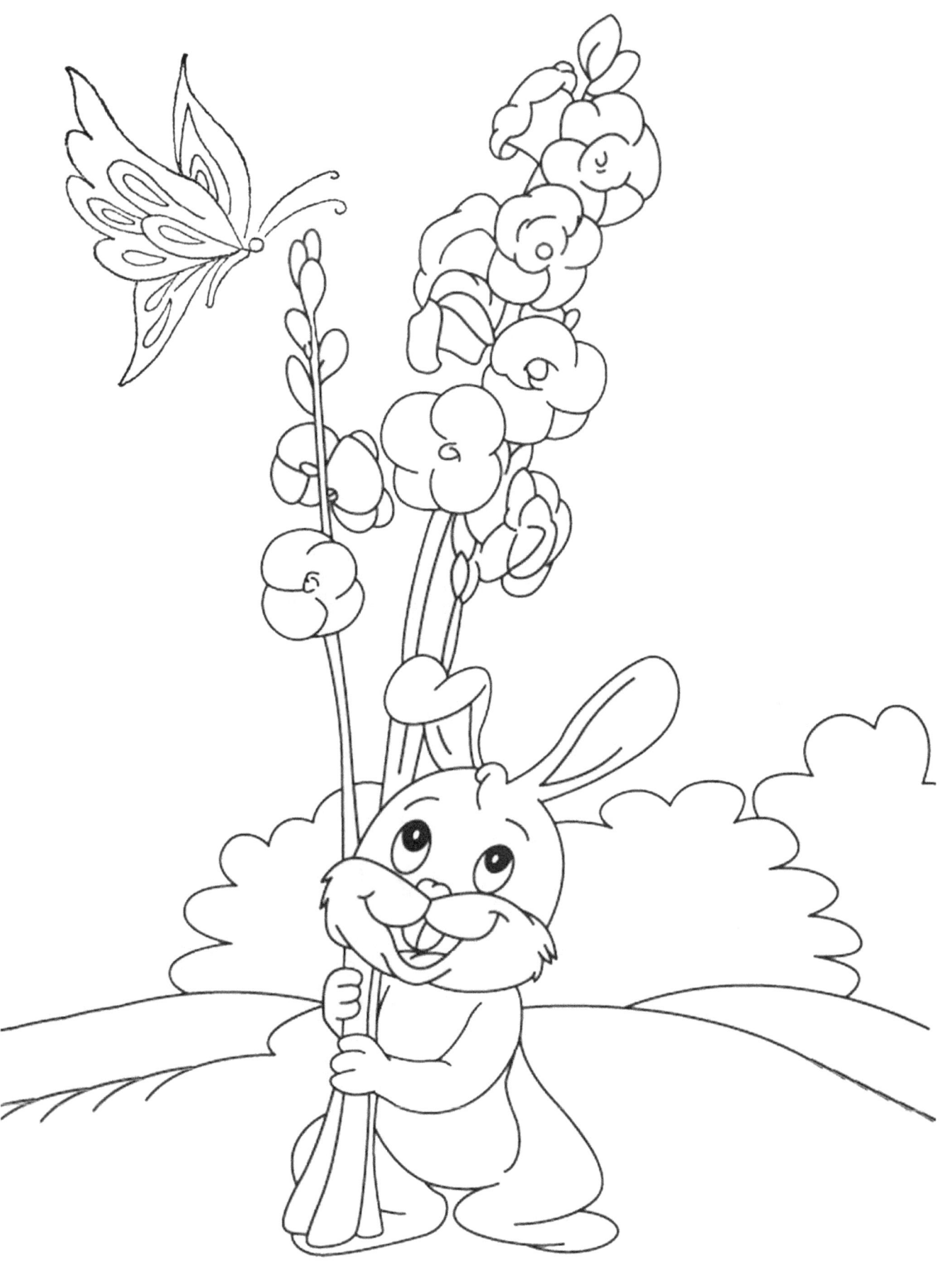

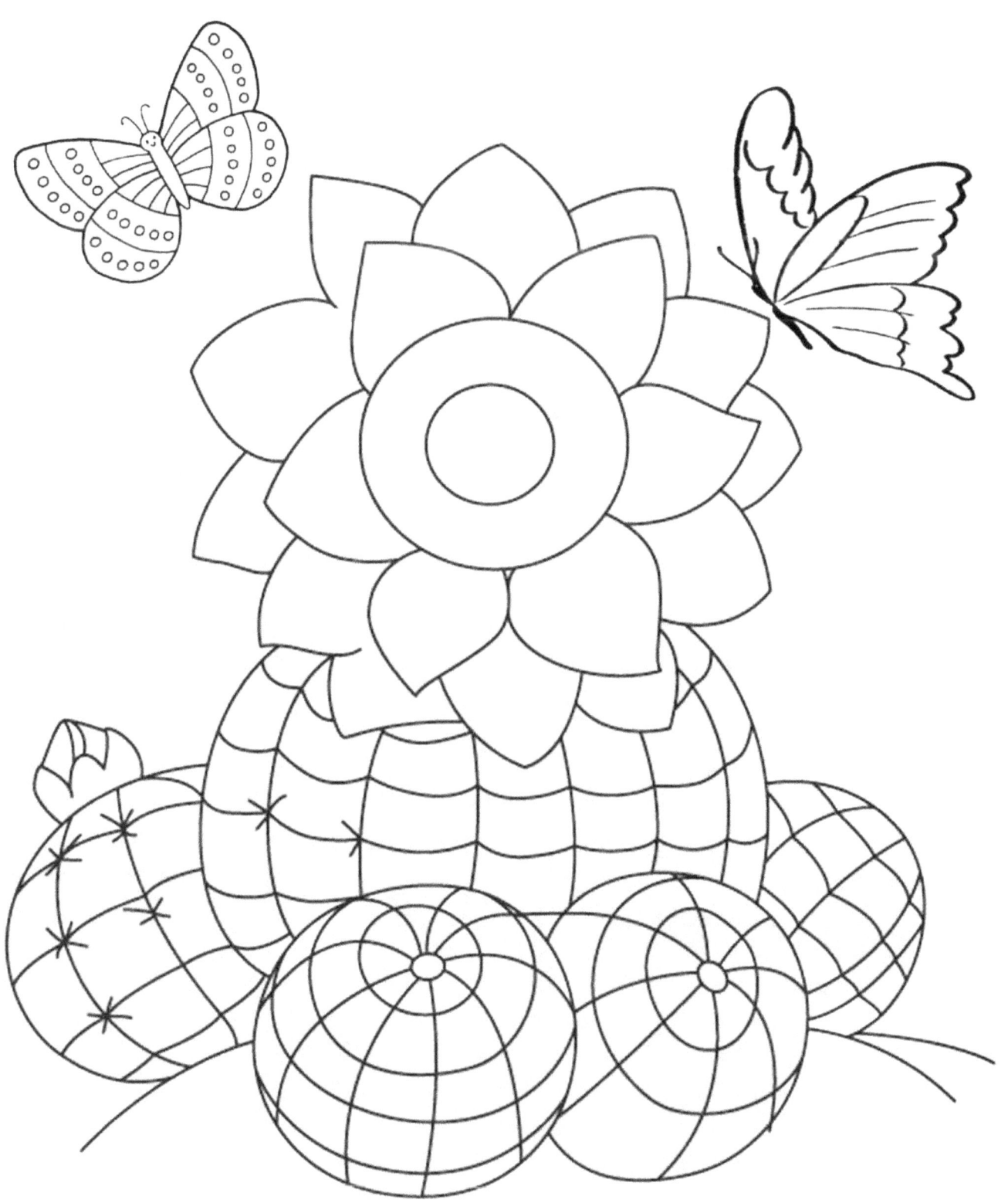

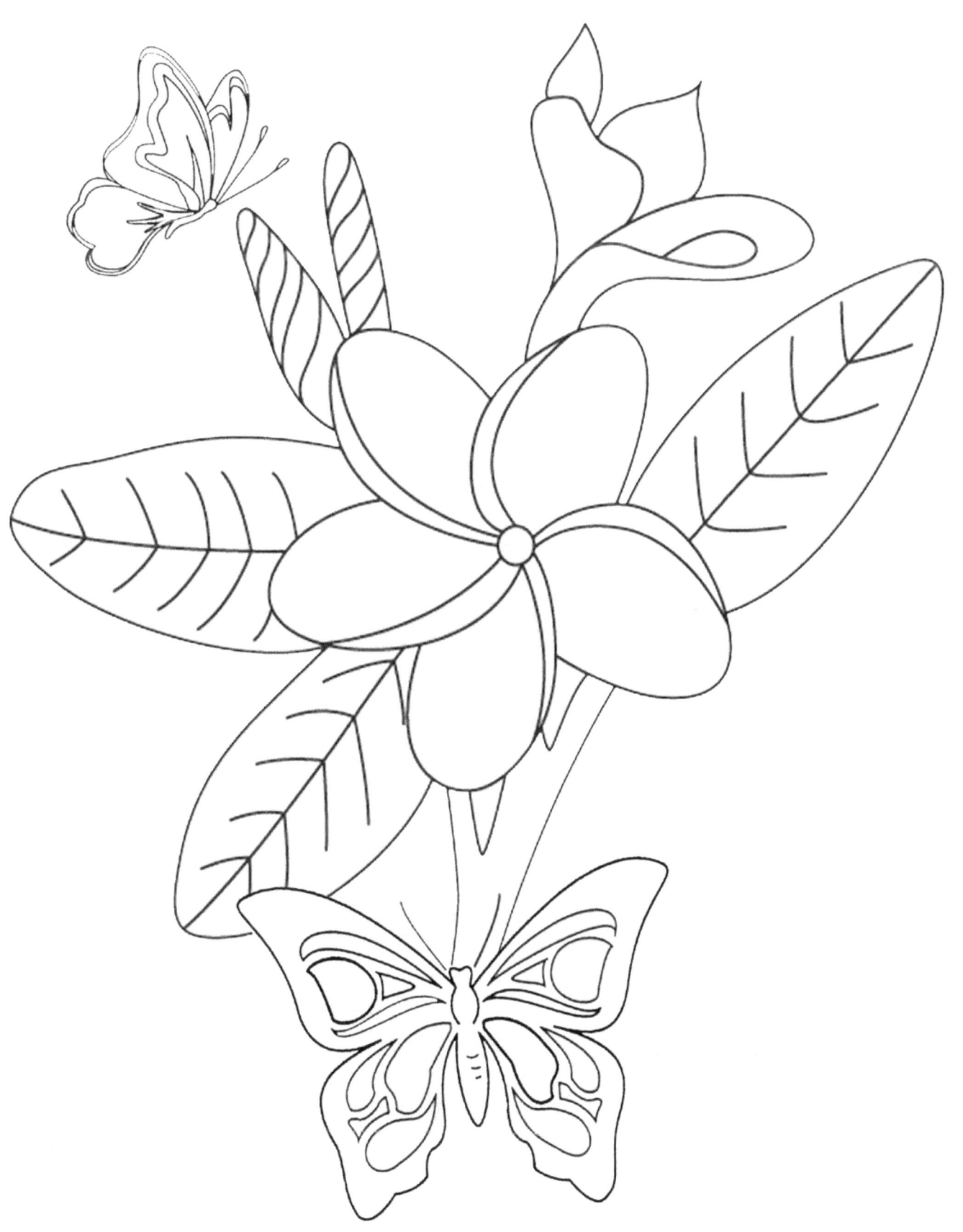

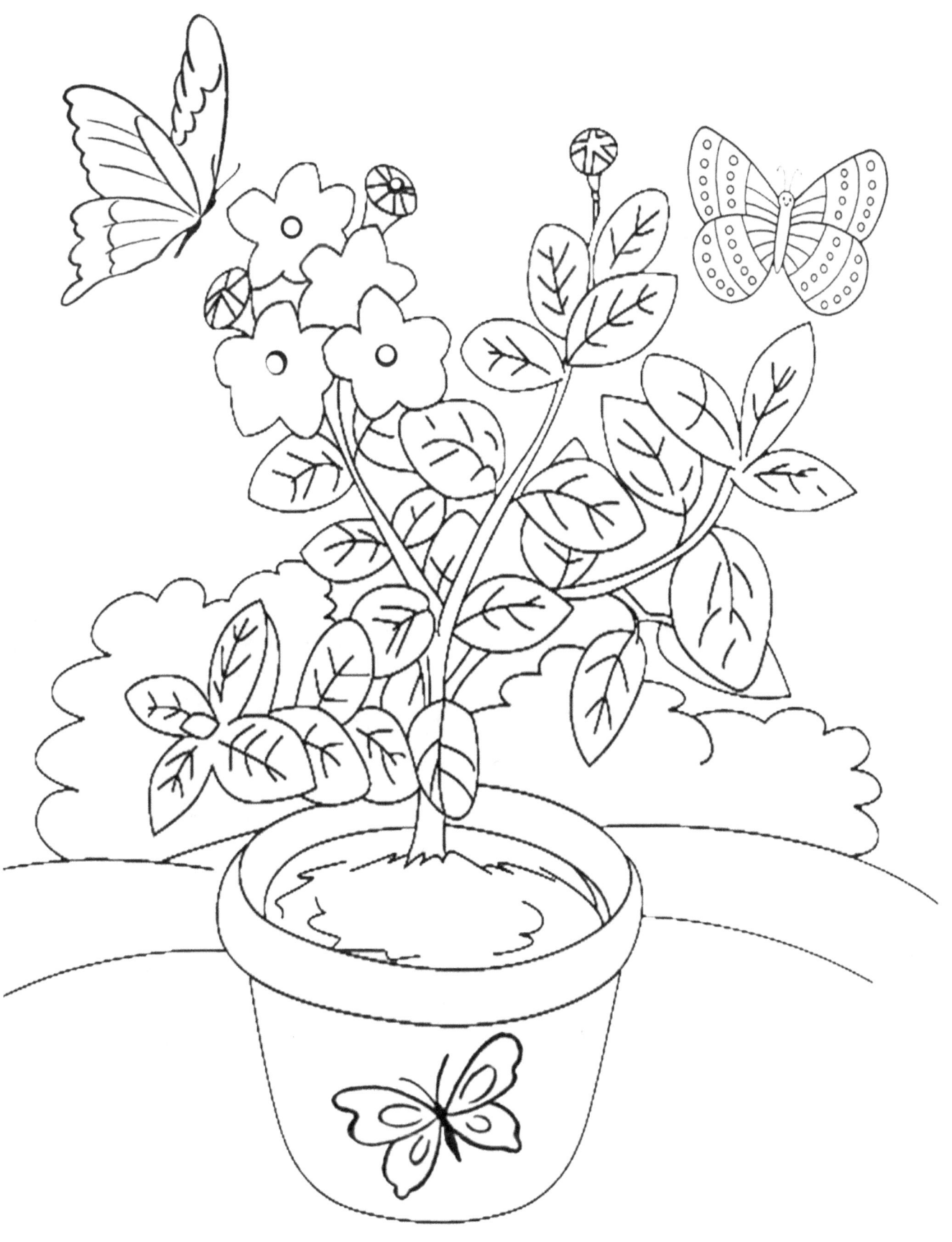

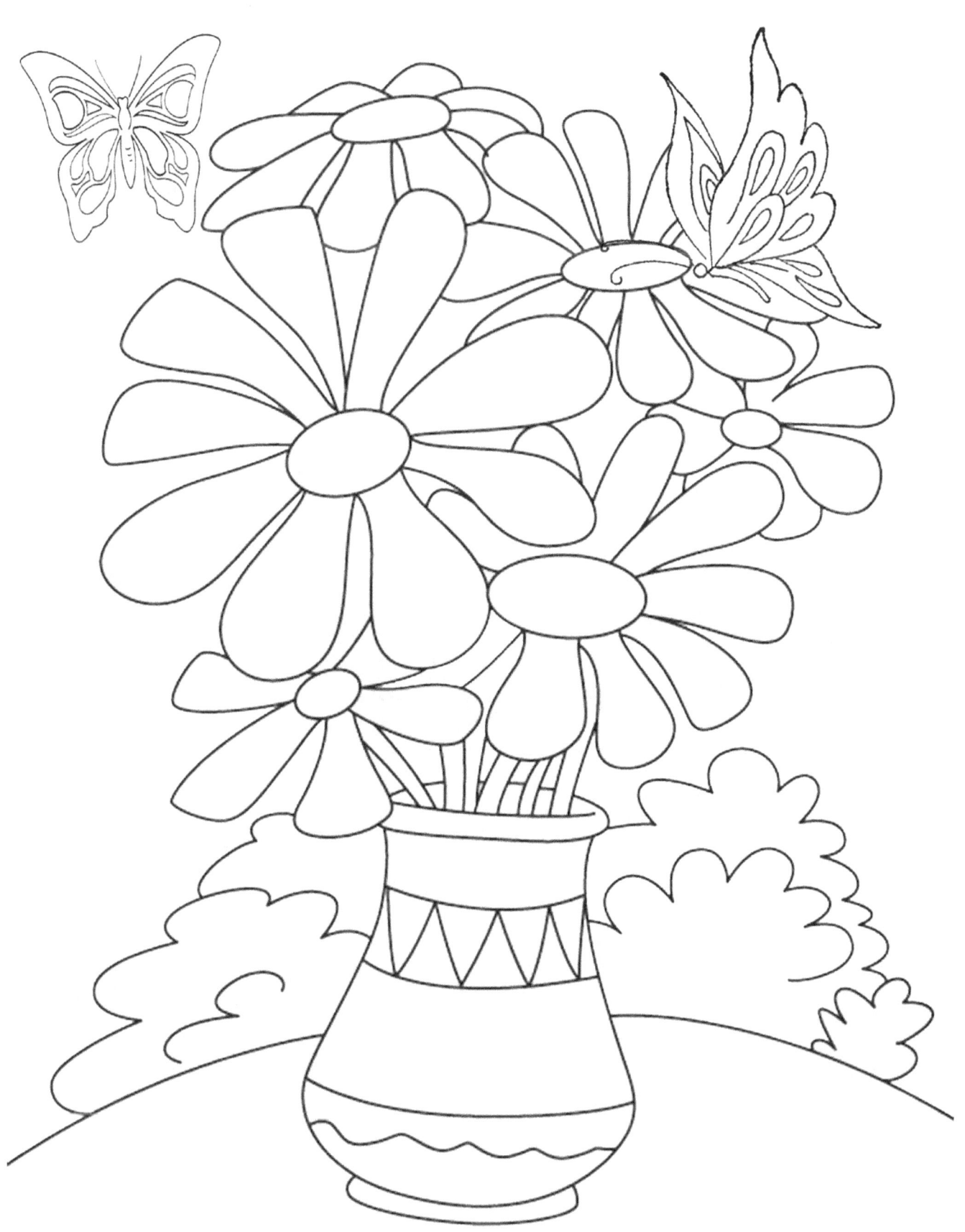

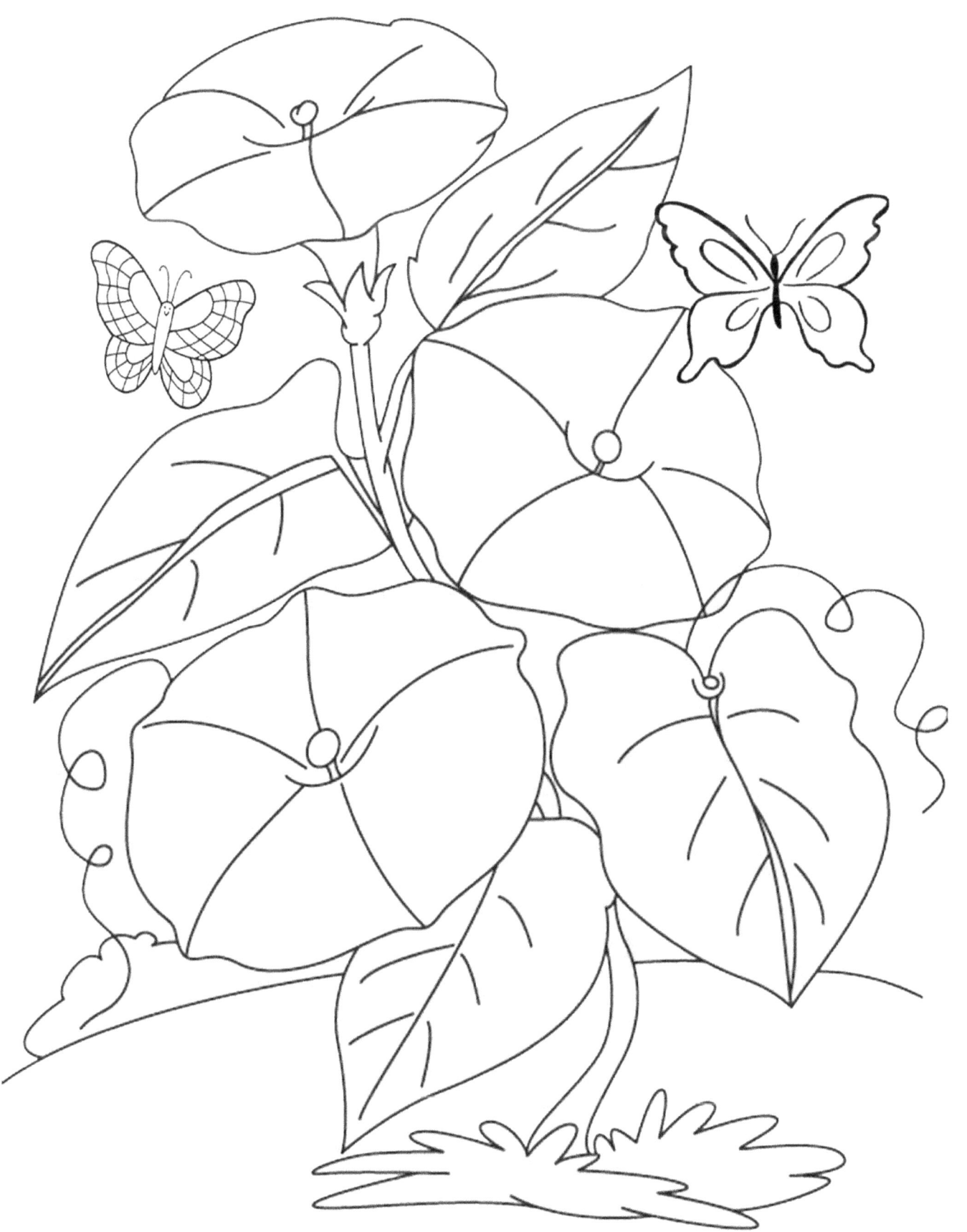

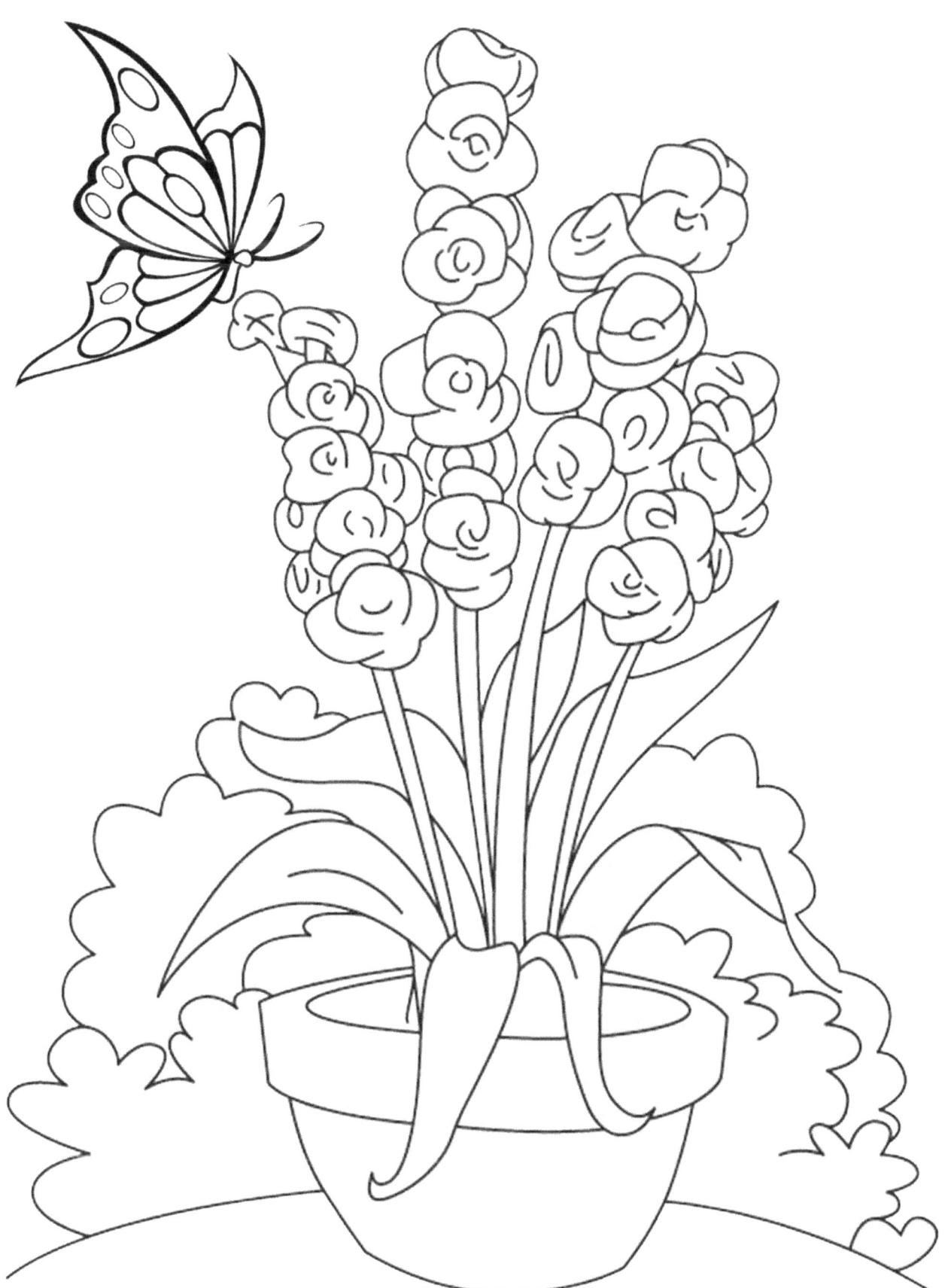

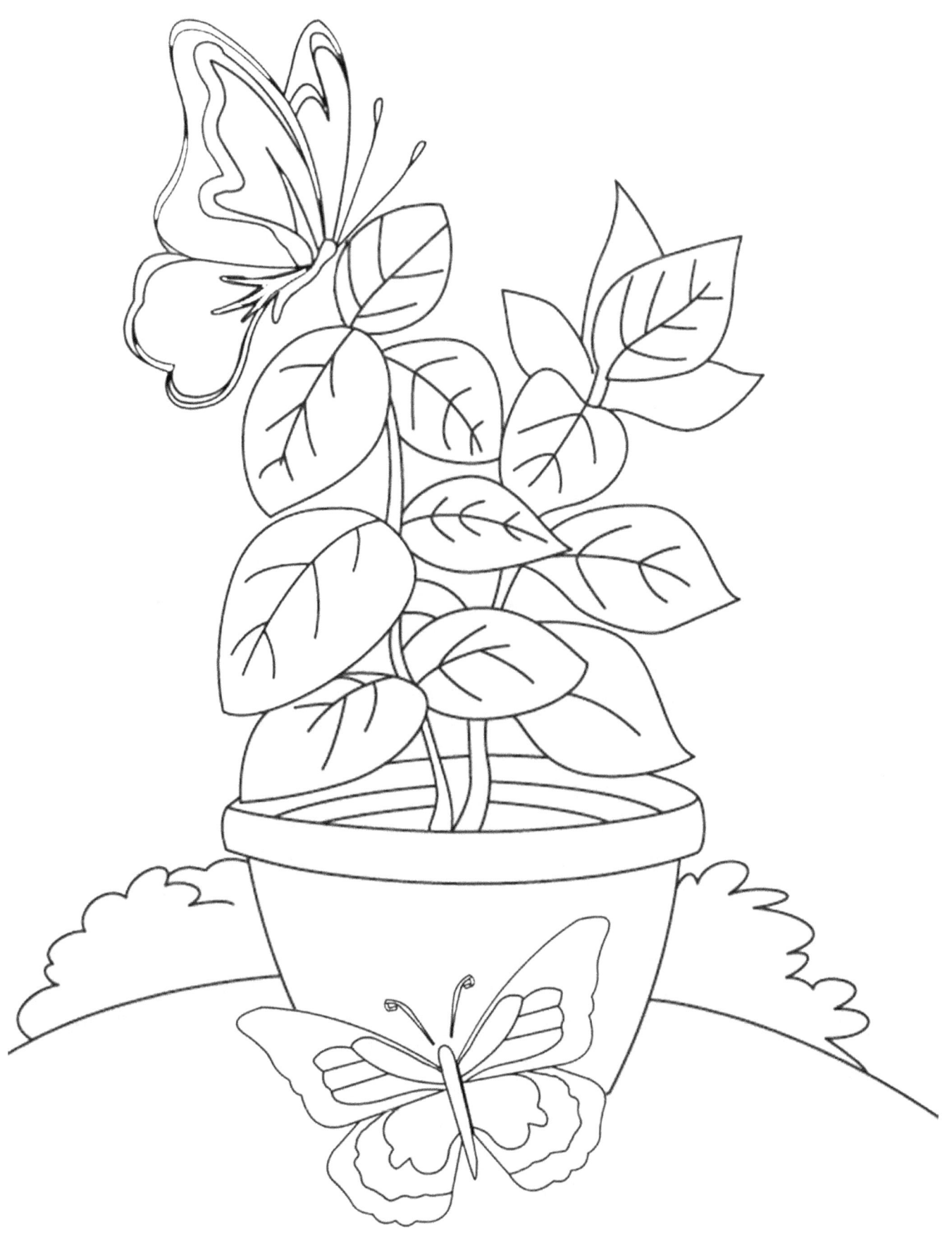

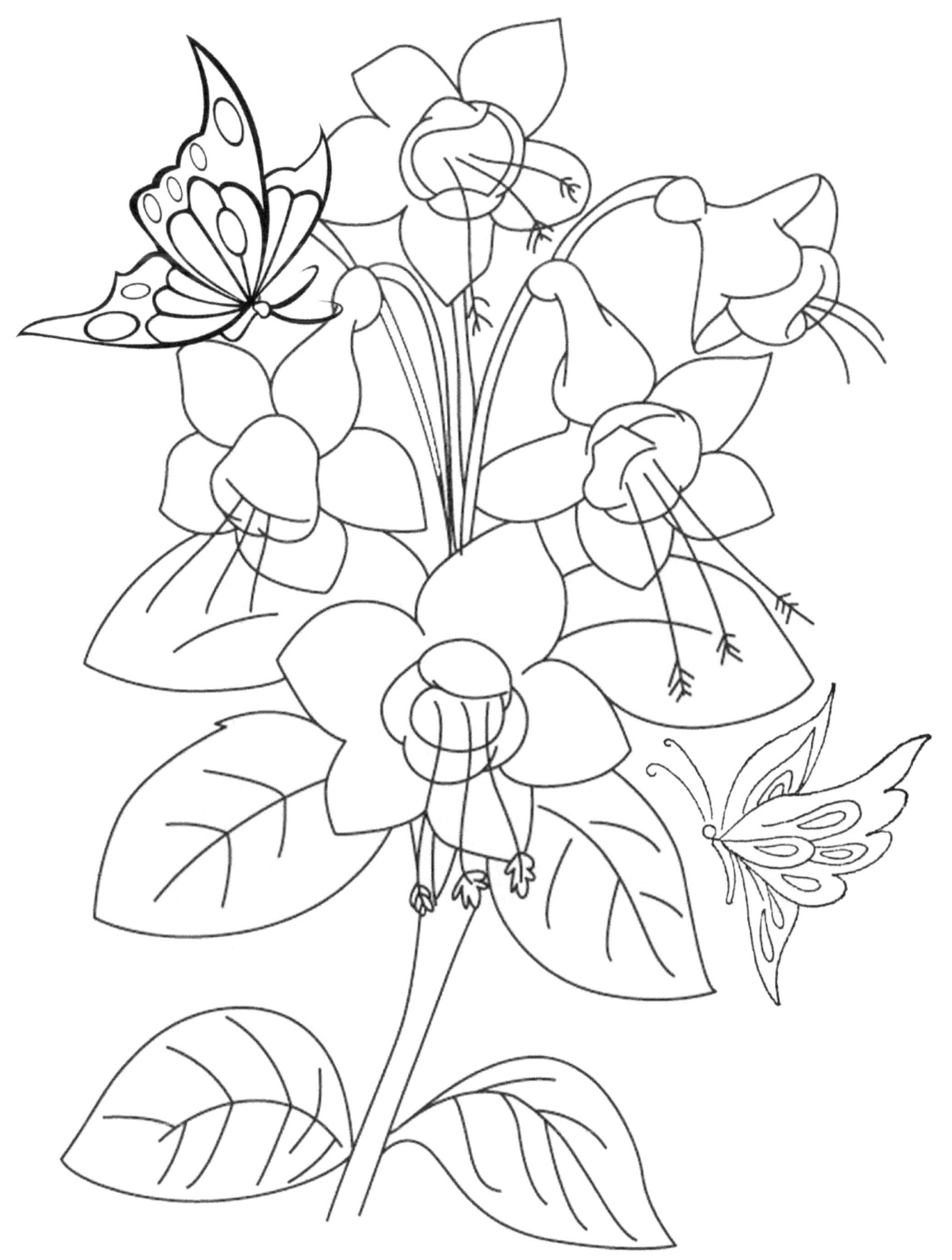

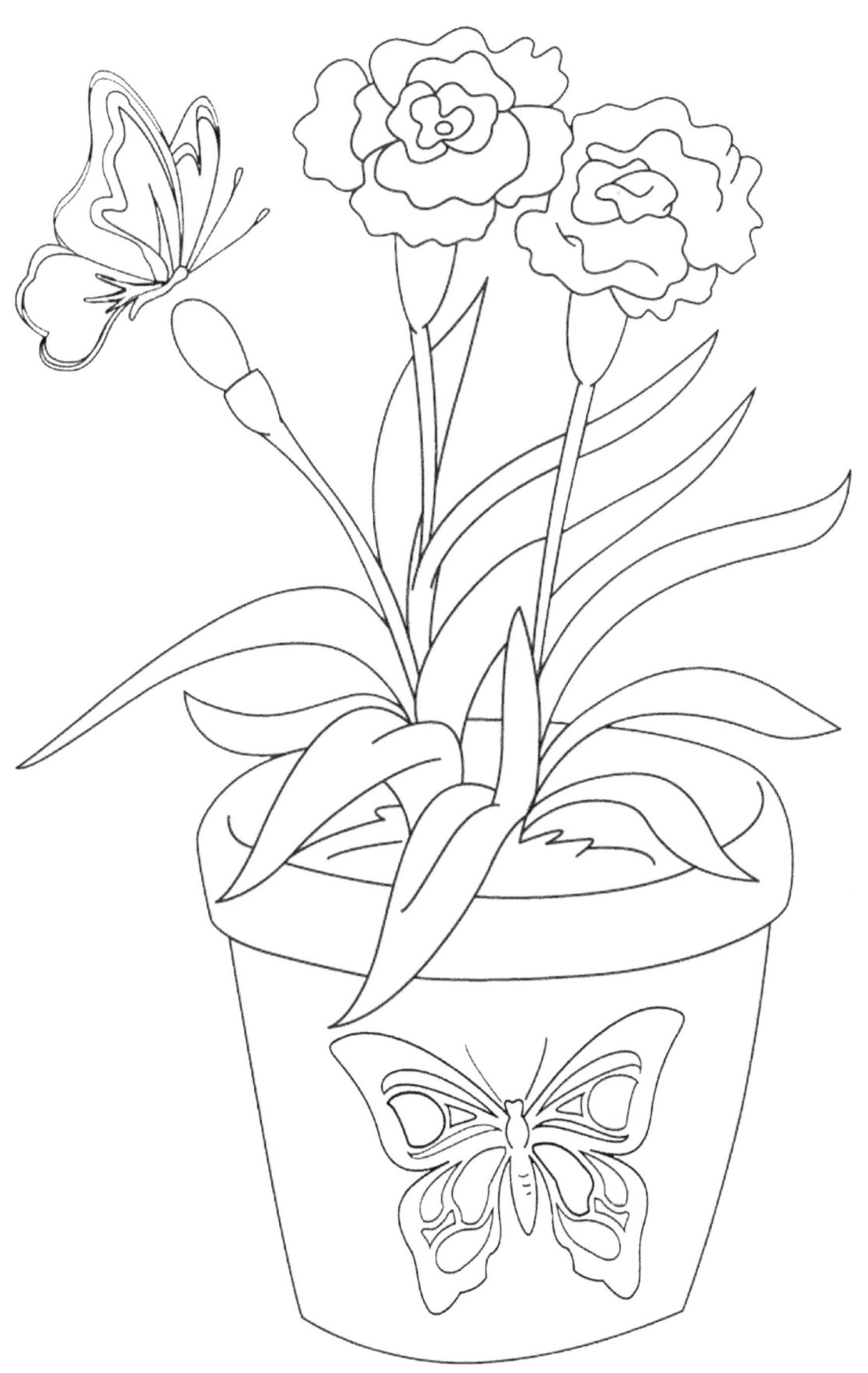

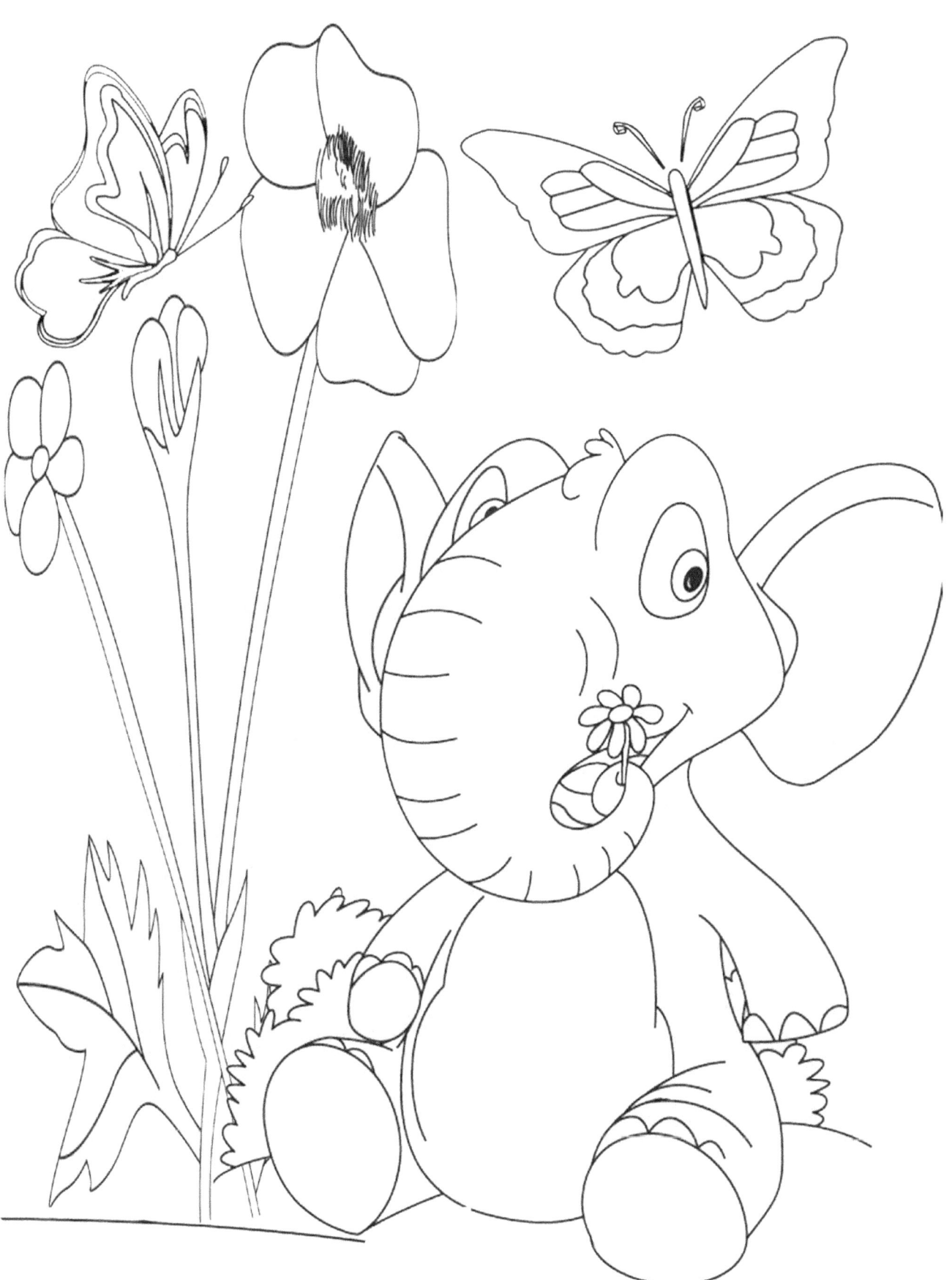

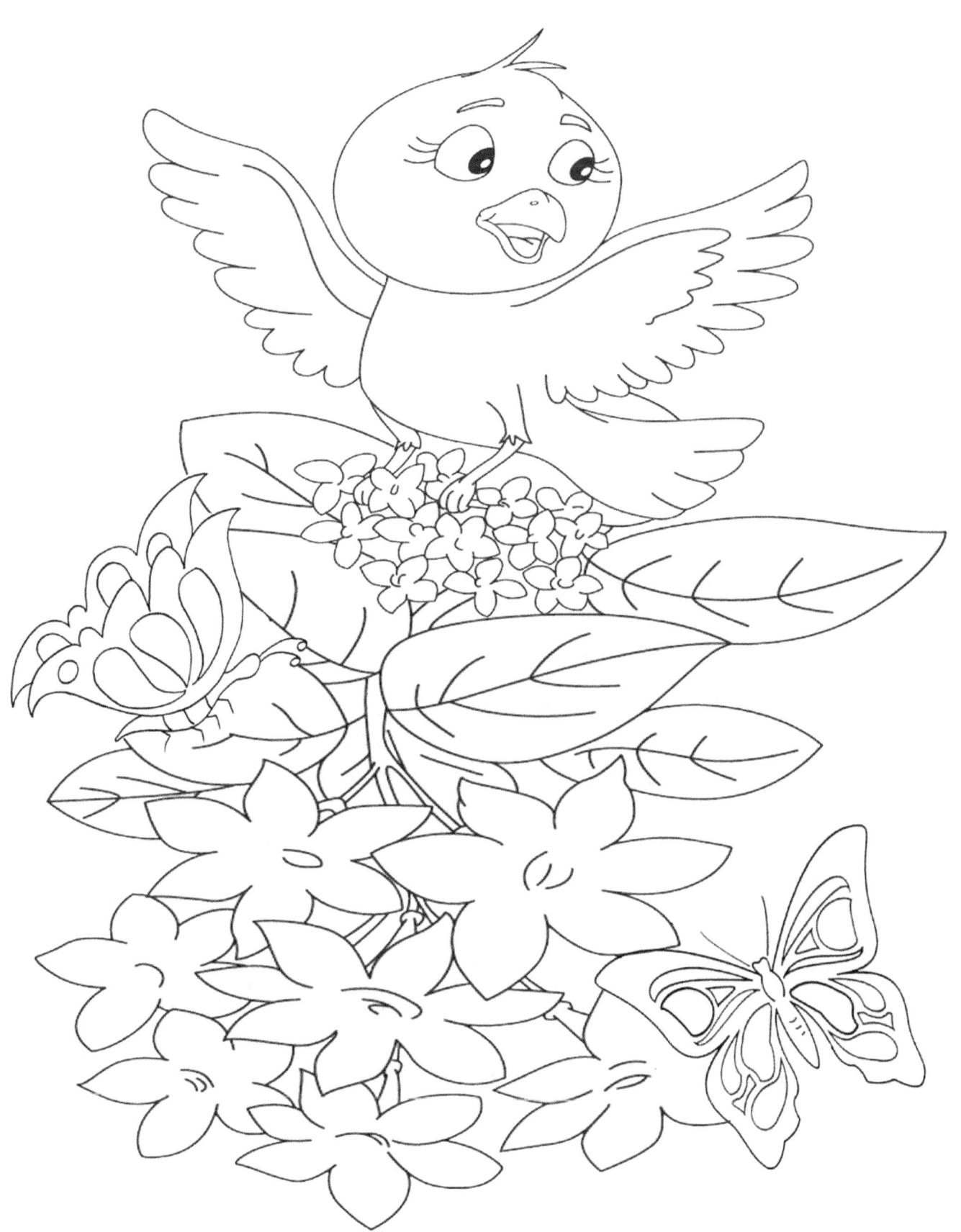

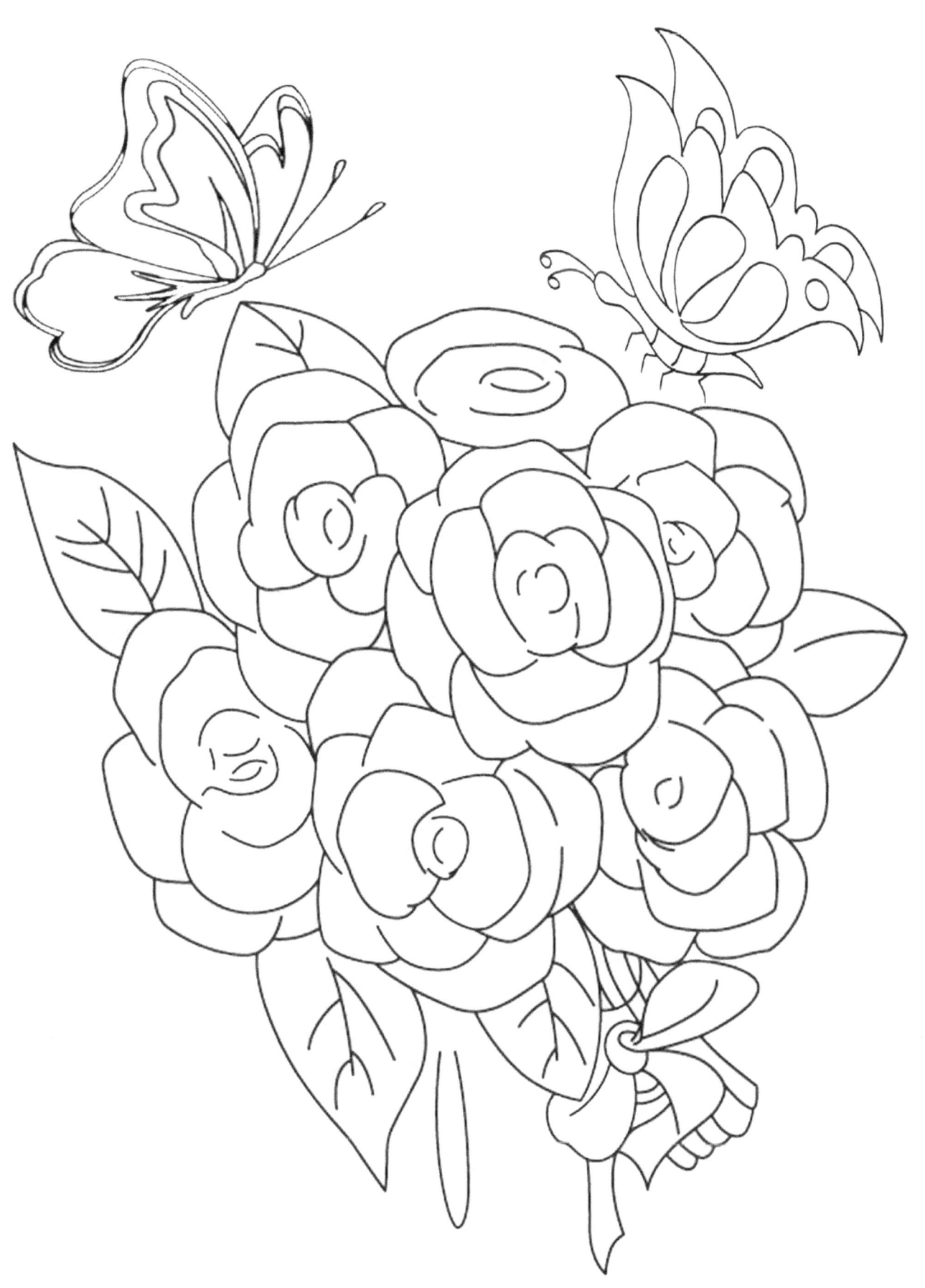

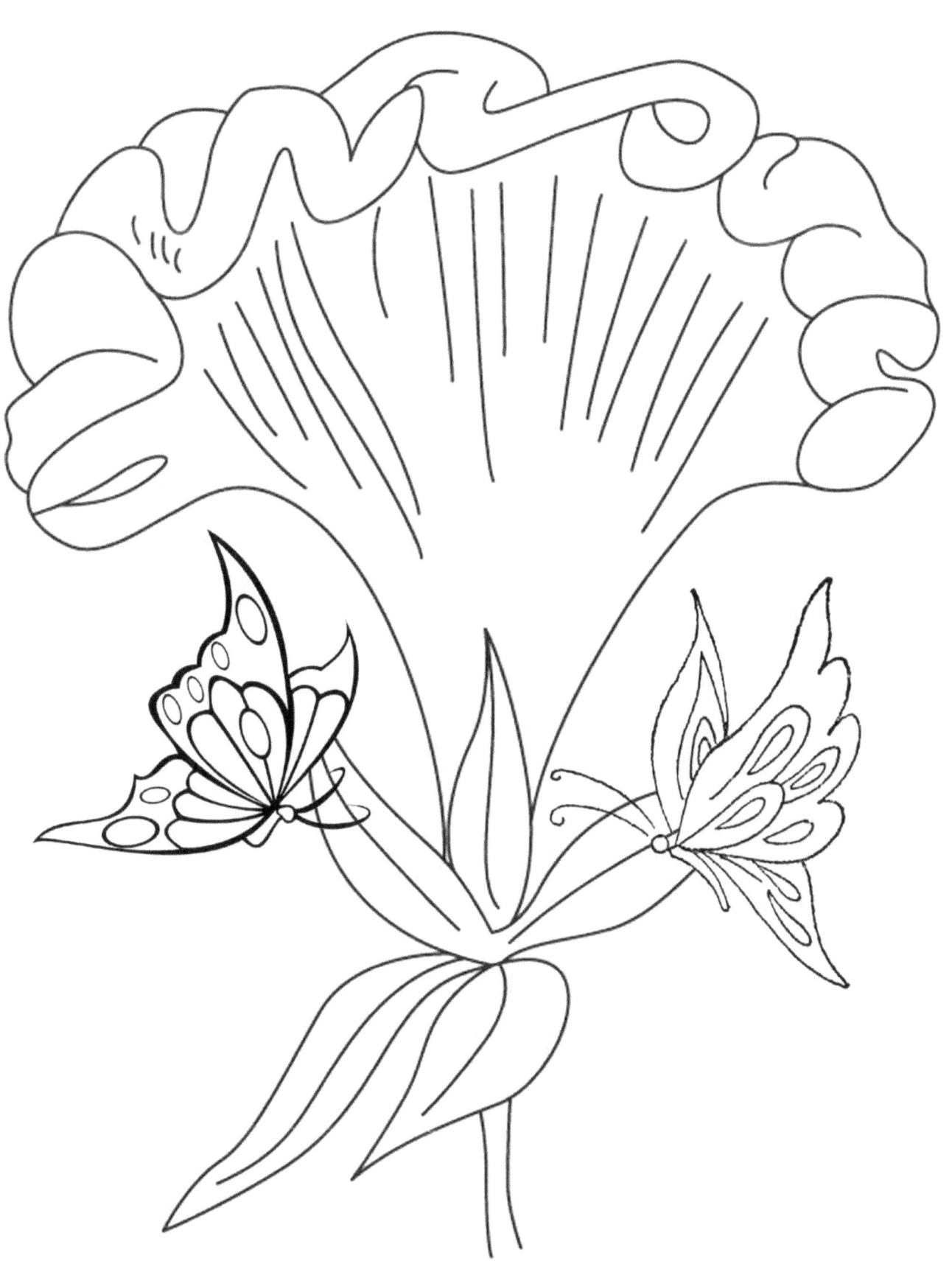

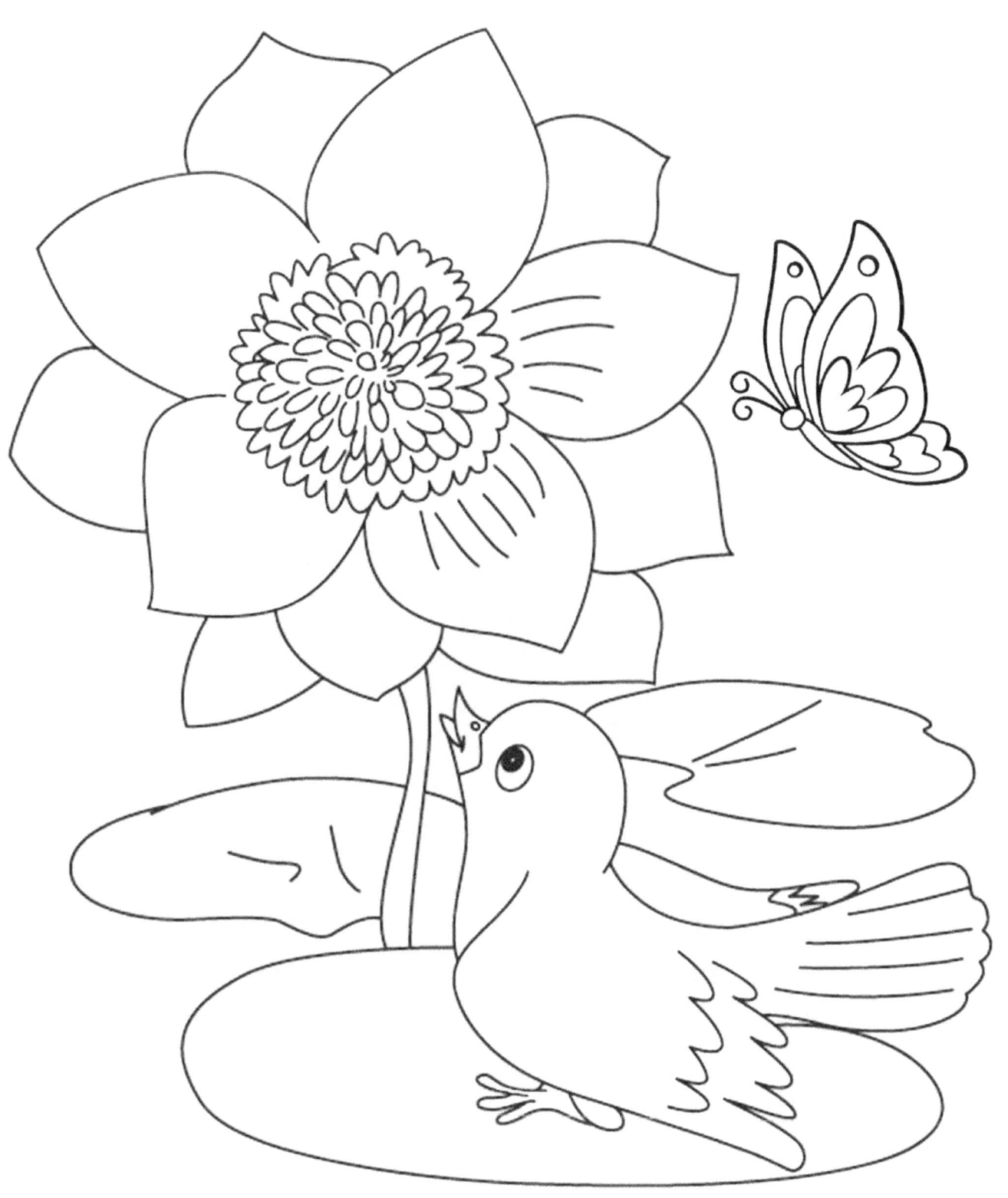

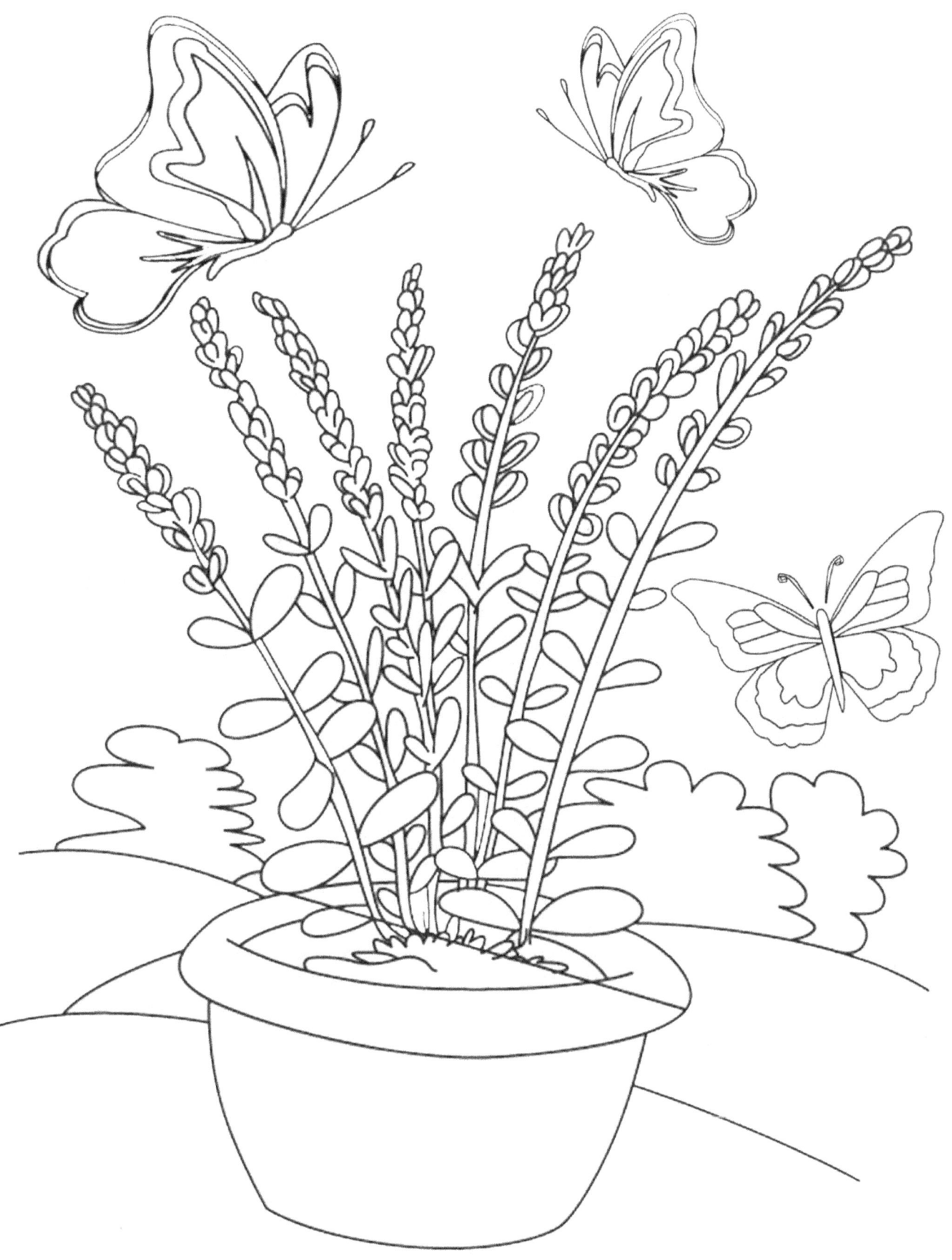

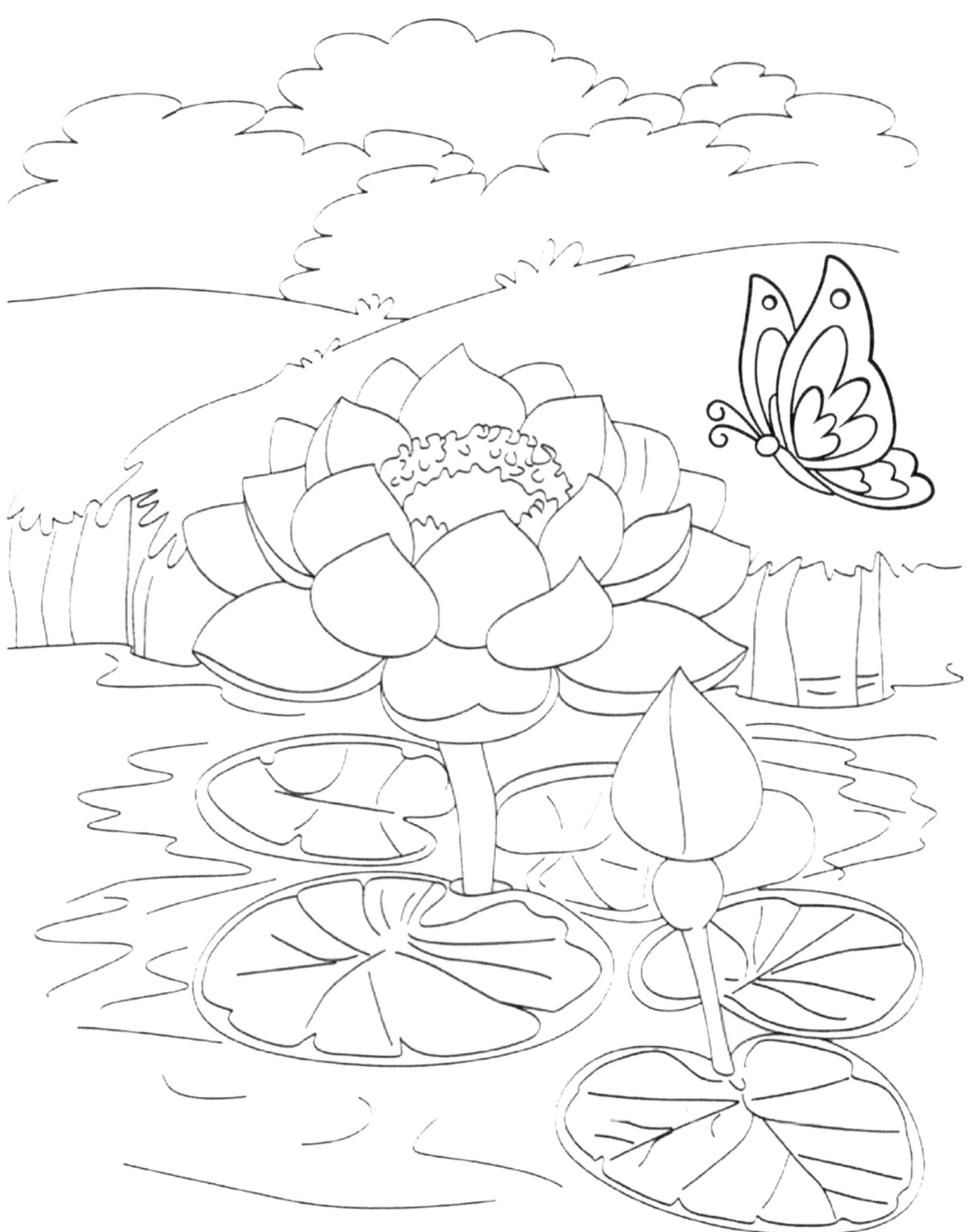

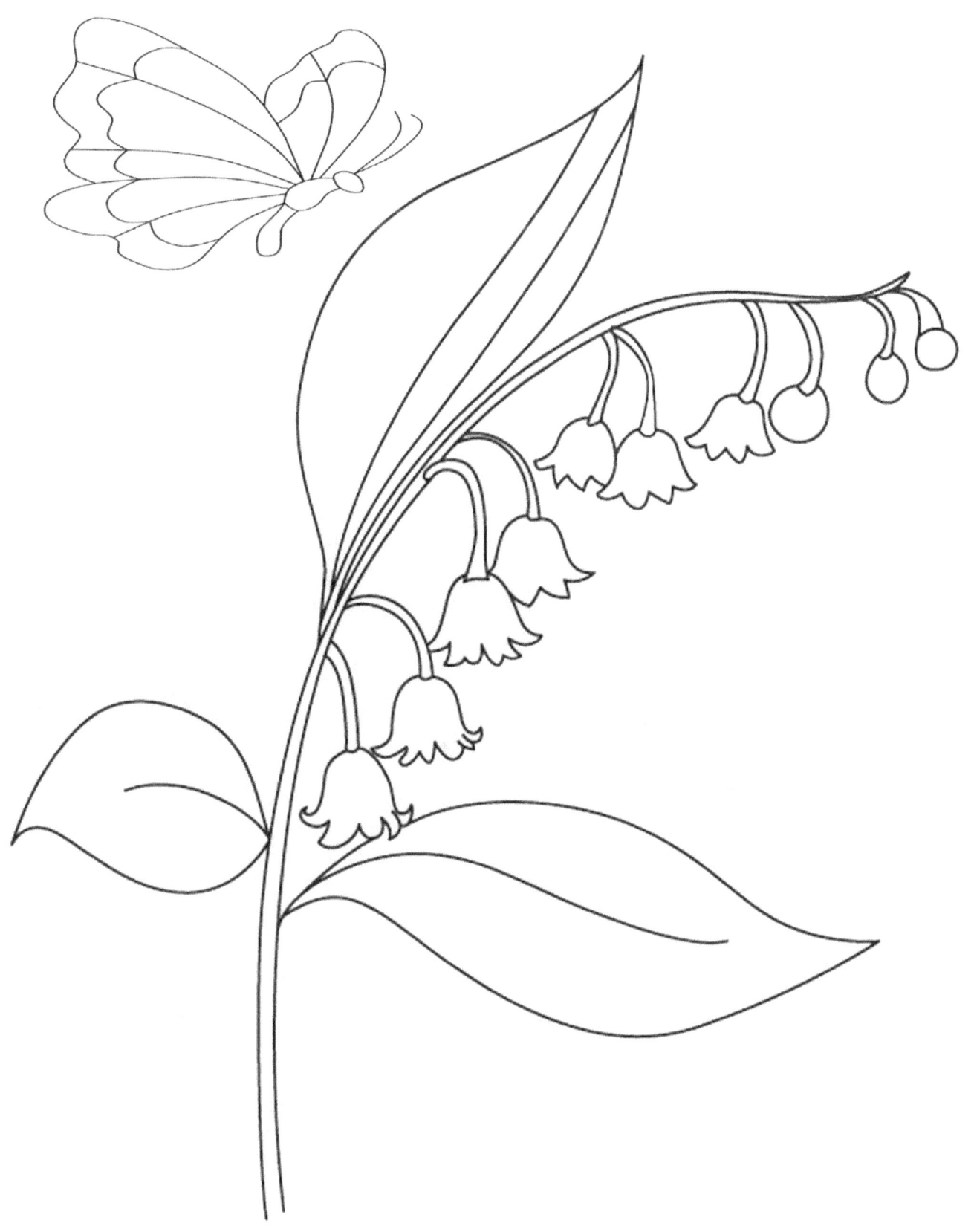

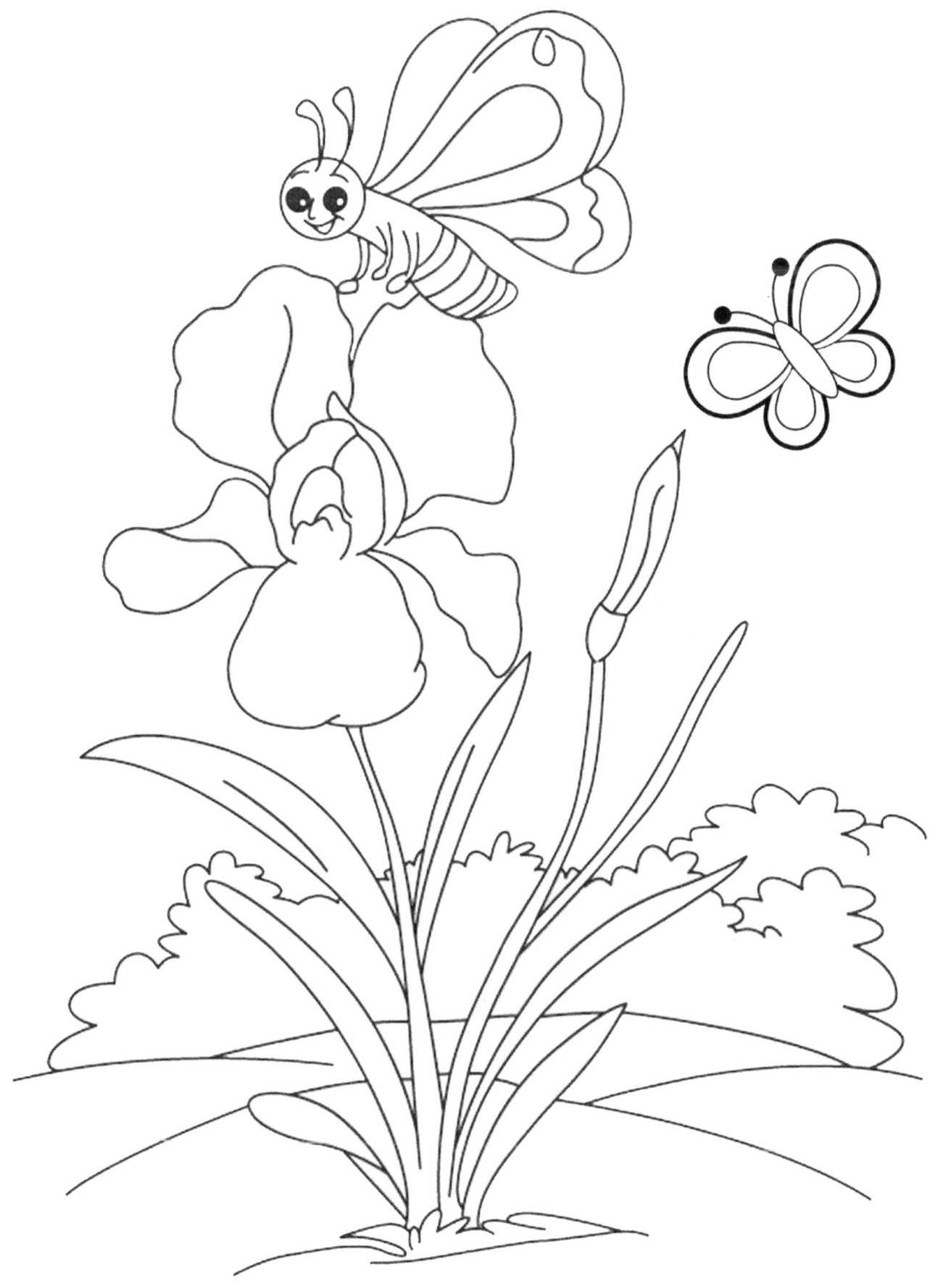

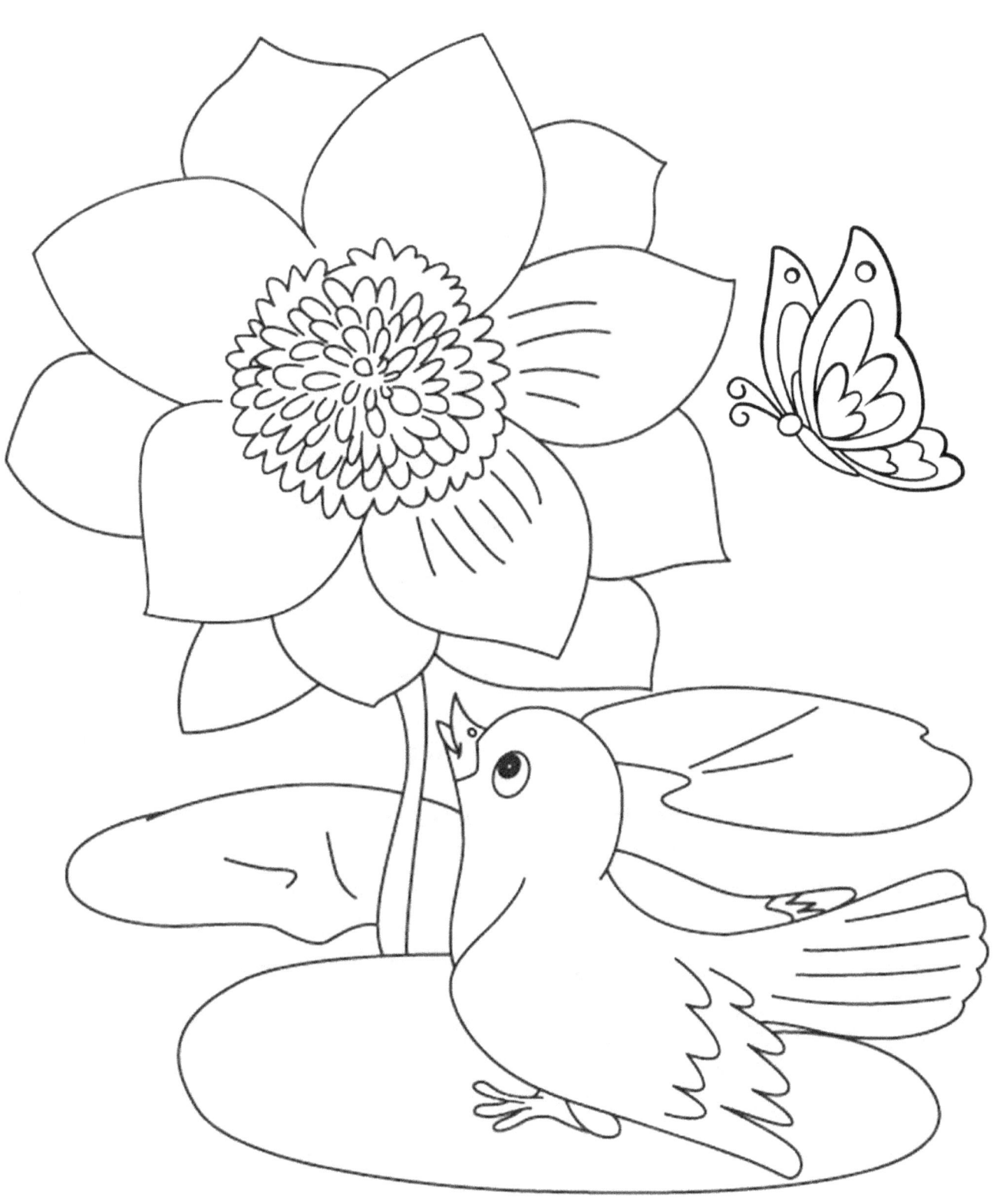

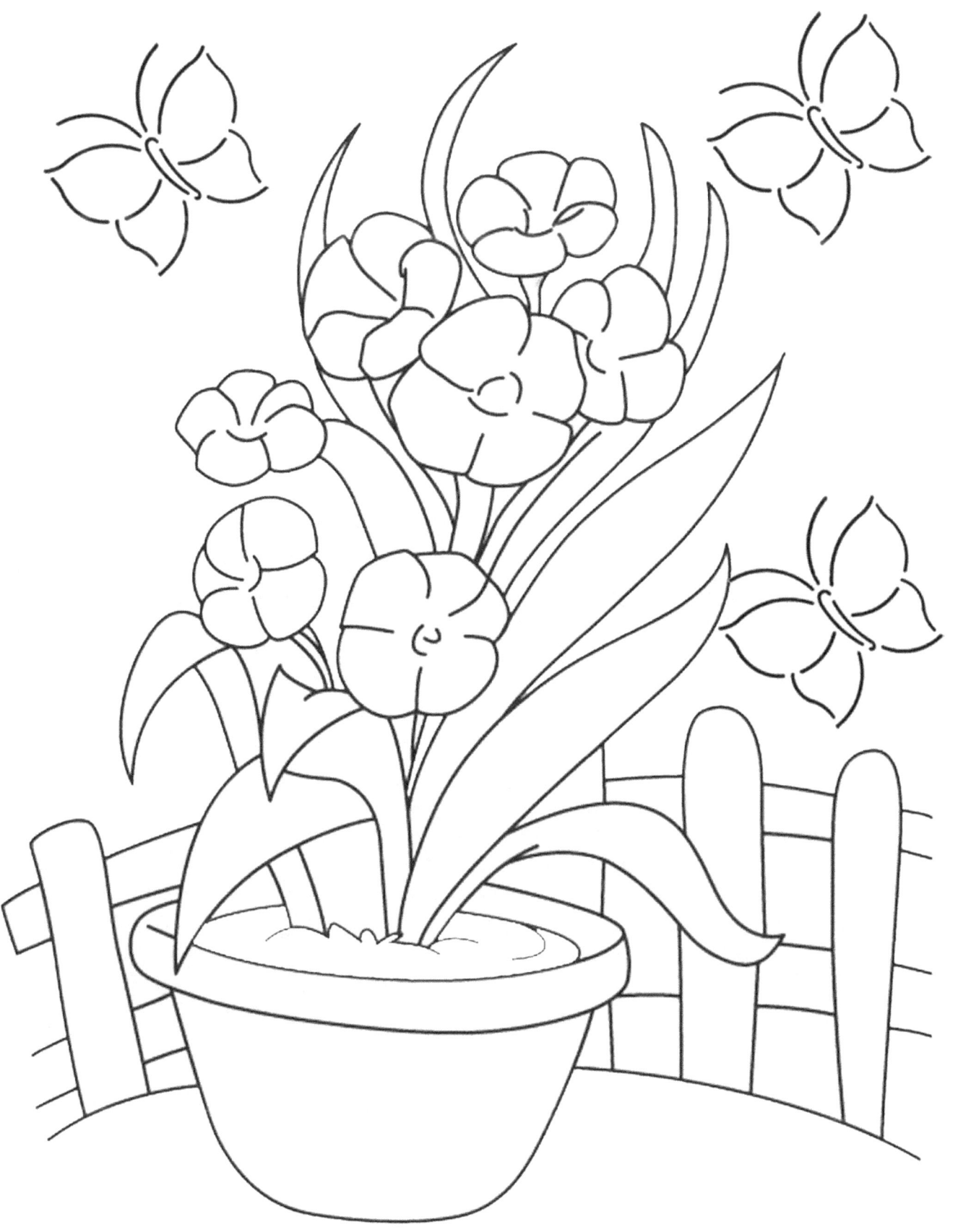

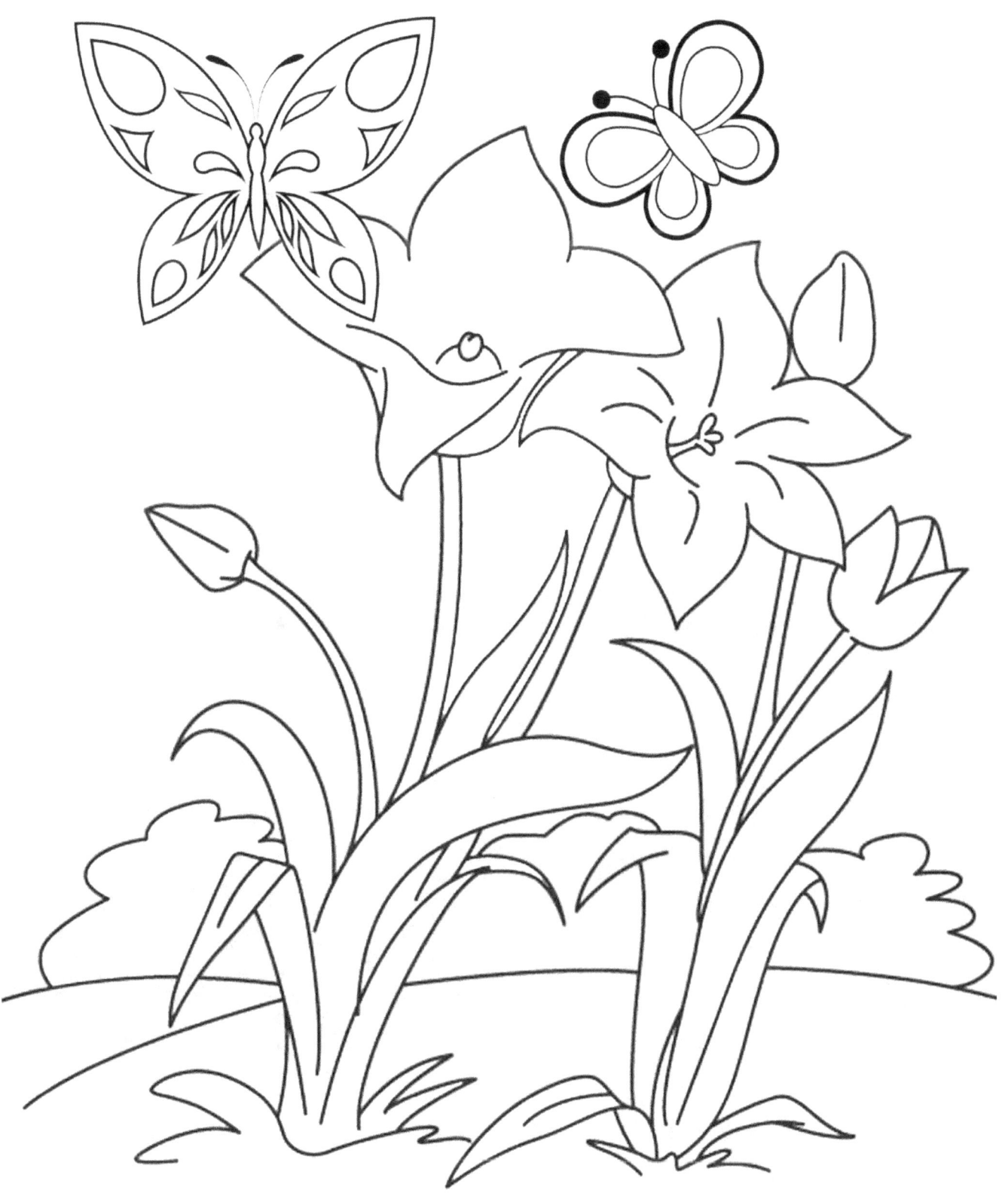

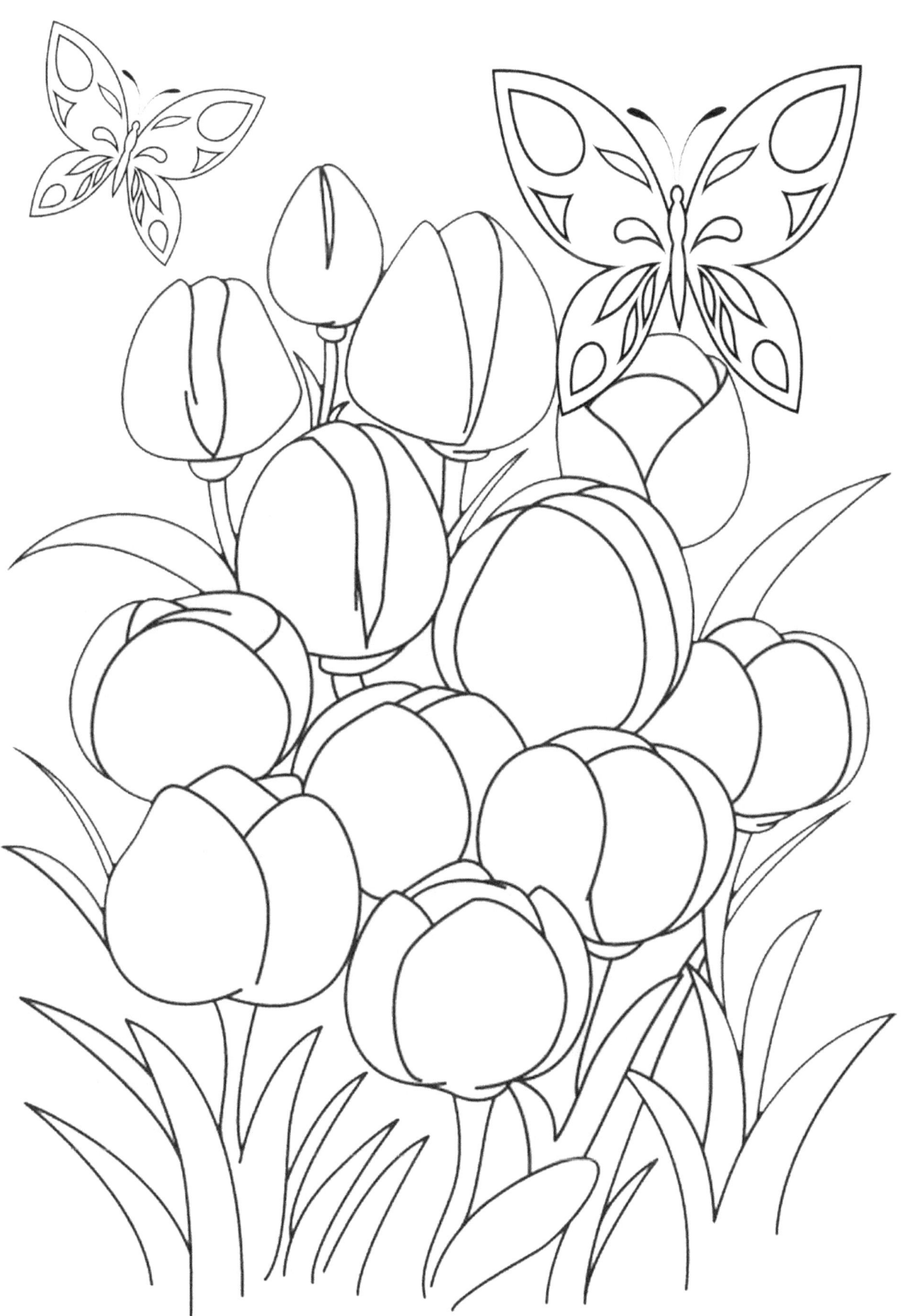

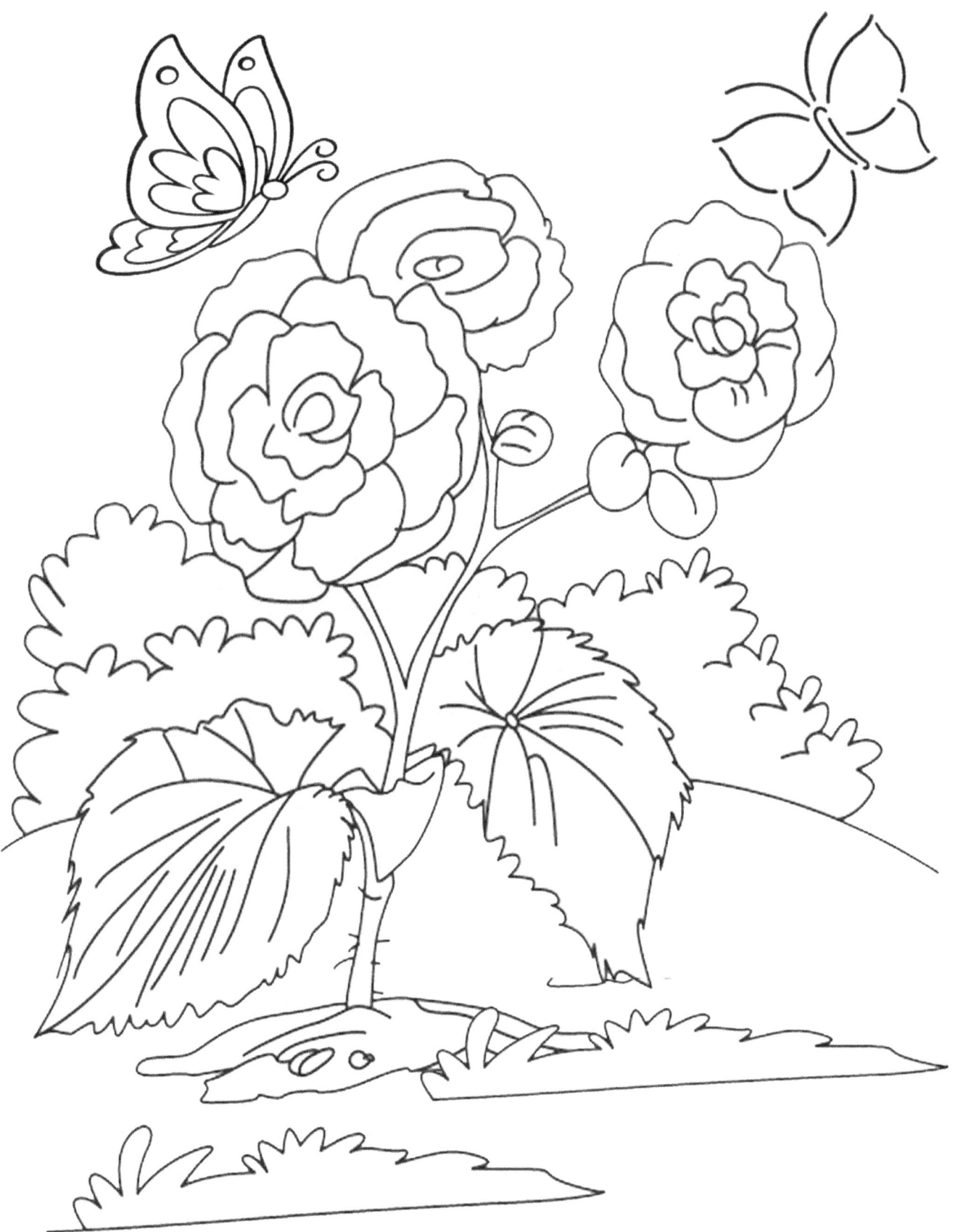

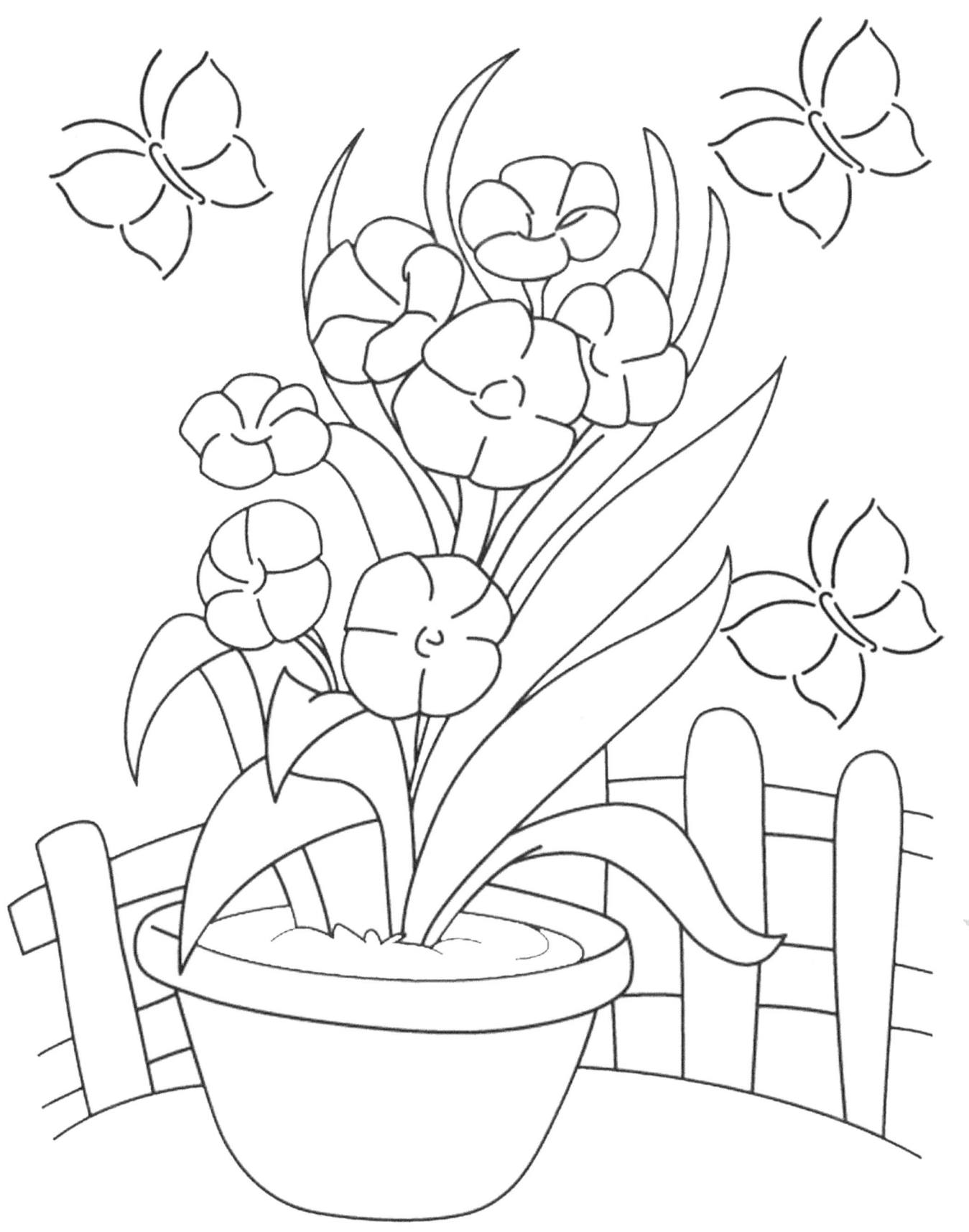

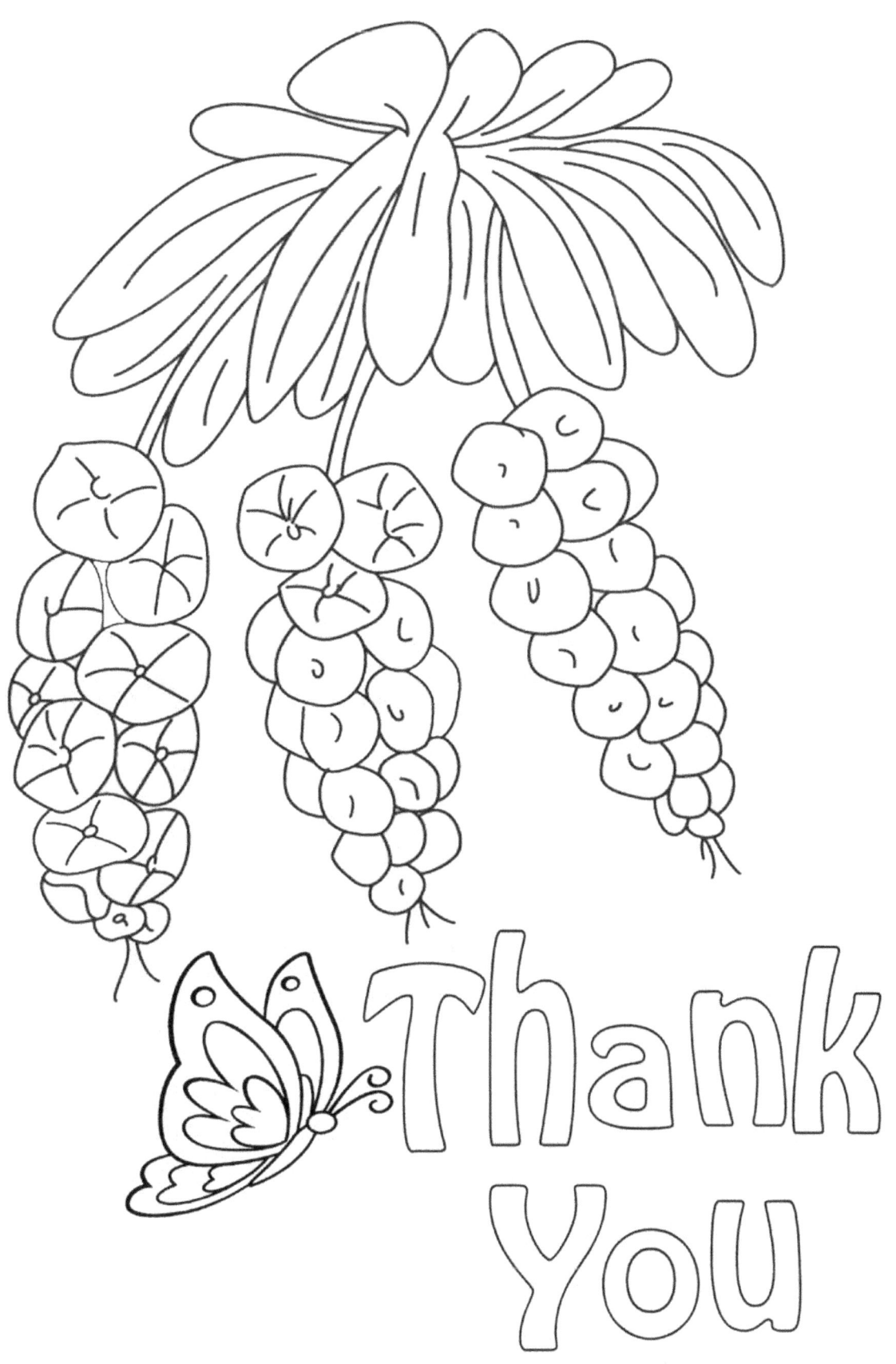

www.ingramcontent.com/pod-product-compliance
Lightning Source LLC
Chambersburg PA
CBHW081613220526

45468CB00010B/2863